BUSINESS HEROES

That's a brilliant idea, but how could it possibly work in my organization?

How often do you think as you read a business book that if only you could ask the author one simple question you could transform your organization?

Capstone is creating a unique partnership between authors and readers, delivering for the first time in business book publishing a genuine after-sales service for book buyers. Simply e-mail Capstone at **capstone_publishing@msn.com** to leave your question (with details of the date and place of purchase of *Business Heroes*) and Sandy Dunlop will try to answer it.

Capstone authors travel and consult extensively so we do not promise an immediate turnaround. Nevertheless, that one question answered might just jump-start your company and your career.

Capstone is more than a publisher. It is an electronic clearing house for pioneering business thinking, putting the creators of new business ideas in touch with the people who use them.

BUSINESS HEROES

Making Business Renewal
Your Personal Crusade

SANDY DUNLOP

ODYSSEY

CAPSTONE

First published 1997 by
Capstone Publishing Limited
Oxford Centre for Innovation
Mill Street
Oxford OX2 0JX
United Kingdom

British Library Cataloguing in Publication Data
A CIP catalogue record for this book is available from the British
Library

ISBN 1-900961-36-9

Typeset in 10/13 pt Palatino by
Sparks Computer Solutions, Oxford
http://www.sparks.co.uk
Printed and bound in Great Britain by
T.J. International Ltd, Padstow, Cornwall

This book is printed on acid-free paper

CONTENTS

PREFACE

Behind every major corporate success there is invariably an untold story. There are many who try to claim the credit for what is now working and proven. But usually there was someone (or some small group) who conceived of and fought for change long before it was popular or profitable.

These people are truly Business Heroes. This book attempts to capture their story. It does so using the framework of the ancient, universal story of 'The Hero's Journey'. These ancient tales, which have certainly stood the test of time, point to a wisdom that is eternal.

This book is for two groups of people. It is for the 'heroes' themselves, offering some advice from the wisdom of ancient myth on how to survive, even thrive, in a world that tends to remove its heroes. It is also for modern leaders and managers who need to renew their organizations in order to survive. For them, more important than all the rhetoric of innovation and change is the special ability to recognize and cherish the few heroes in their midst who might just help them through. A hero judges leaders on their actions, not their words!

ACKNOWLEDGEMENTS AND CREDITS

This book has been a long time in the writing, and even longer in the thinking. It is the kind of work that must grow out of experience. The words must have been lived and felt. So I have to go back to a week in the Dublin mountains some 15 years ago when Paul Rebillot, actor and musician, led us through the ritual and story of The Heroes Journey. All through the years Joseph Campbell's Esalen tapes on world mythology and his books have been a constant companion. I only ever heard the great Campbell and saw him on video but there is no doubt he was an 'experience'.

Exploring Homer and fifth-century Athens via the Open University courses and guides who truly love and live that time was a joy. Thank you Wesley Semple, Simon Spence and Aideen Hartney. Lucy Collins did the same for the literature of Joyce, Yeats and Becket. In terms of the writing, what matters is who believes in you and the thoughts when there's nothing very readable. Noel Jones, early on, Eleanor Ash later, always seemed to believe. And with the very early drafts, Pat McCaffrey, Fergus Balfour and Maurice O'Grady struggled through and pointed ways forward. Jane Frost and Deirdre Simpson worked repeatedly on the re-drafts and re-drafts.

Storytelling has some substance when based on the events of the everyday – making the ordinary extraordinary. There are many corporate 'heroes' and 'warriors' you meet while consulting over the years; they were part of shaping the experiences and ideas that built this book. To all of them, many thanks.

In terms of reading the later version of the book, however, Richard Holmes and Jacqui Mees were very helpful, encouraging and open to the power of the non-rational. And James Ryan (the secret author!) and Caroline Walsh, who wondered how business had managed to bypass for so long so much of what was happening in the world of literature and cultural criticism. That meal in Aghaboe was a special nudge along the road!

The Synectics Company have also been terrific. Thanks Vincent for the job. And those heady days of the late 1970s in Church Street, Harvard Square, Cambridge and Church Lane, Euston, London and John A., Jason, John E. and Rick, John P., Marvin, Eric and, of course, the great George Prince. Then Barre and the Irish team – more 'heady days' – and in the States, Ned, Ginna, Will, Pam, Peg, Doug and then Roger, Peter (especially on early versions of the book), Michael and the IOU. Spending all that time in creativity 'process' and 'innovation' was so significant.

And now – a new team for work on major brands and on marketing using Archetype, Ritual, Science with Janet French, Bill Felton and all the academics. The Greek gods and goddesses, heroes and heroines live again in yet another promising rebirth, or is it Renaissance? Yes, James Joyce, perhaps history is circular. And, thanks, Jacqui for the support.

Thanks to Anchor Productions, and the two principals, Marguerite Somers and Ellen O'Malley for all the encouragement and help on the details. Thanks to the poets Michael O'Siadhail and Seamus Heaney for permission to use a few lines of their poetry

Finally and most importantly, the two who have been with the project from conception to delivery: my wife, Ellen, and my mother, Esther. This is for them.

1
MYTH ON THE BOTTOM LINE

The Audacious Challenge

Watch over us in our troubles
O saga of all that has happened
If we must be such wanderers
– Michael O'Siadhail

CONTENTS

- Introduction
- The Wisdom of Myth
- The Players in the Kingdom
- Framework of the Book
- Theoretical Context

INTRODUCTION

Whenever an individual or a group of individuals embarks on a mission of radical innovation or change, they are by definition embarking on a journey into new and uncharted territory. They are also setting in play forces and energies which are very difficult to predict or control, and which if they are not careful, may seriously undermine, if not altogether defeat, their intended mission. These forces and energies can be more powerful than any system, structure or procedure set up to contain them. They are the forces of 'chaos' out of which, hopefully, in time, creativity and change will emerge triumphant.

The purpose of this book is to explore the corporate journey of these creative individuals. We look on them as heroes, and their task, we will see, is indeed heroic.

The word 'hero' is used here advisedly. The word itself carries with it a certain amount of baggage. It is often associated with the term 'star' and equated with film stars or the characters they portray, e.g. Indiana Jones, Superman, Terminator. The corporate 'hero' to which we will be attending is not a 'superman', in this sense. He or she is more likely to be reviled than revered, more likely to be feared than adored, and much more likely to withdraw and reflect than to actually seek out public attention.

The hero figure, as we will define the character, is that person who takes the 'lead' in the journey into new and uncharted territories. The 'hero' has definite qualities and characteristics, the defining one being passion. This passion is total, compelling, charismatic and, for certain people, very threatening.

The hero has the capacity to break boundaries and obstacles in a relentless search for the new. Learning and discovery are the primary driving motivations which will lead him or her to that 'big idea', that breakthrough, that paradigm shift. To others this same behaviour will be seen as disruptive; the person may be viewed as a 'troublemaker', dangerous and threatening.

Heroes have high tolerance for ambiguity, paradox, complexity and chaos. They will thrive in times of crisis. They are excellent at initiating innovation and change. And they are not good corporate citizens! Like the Hindu god Shiva, they are creative *and* destructive at the same time.

The 'hero' and the 'heroic' are relatively rare in the modern corporation. Most companies, large and small, could be described as 'warrior' cultures. Most people in senior executive positions are 'warrior' characters.

In fact, it might be argued that the primary organizing image of modern business is that of the warrior. The language managers use is often warrior language, e.g. 'organize the troops', 'into battle', 'casualties', 'attack'. Books which directly use the military metaphor, e.g. Sun Tzu: *War and Management*, are very popular.

Warriors like clarity, clear plans, action. They like setting objectives/goals and getting the people (troops) behind them so that everyone is proceeding in the same direction. They like what is proven and tested. They dislike ambiguity and confusion, and will tend to be intolerant of the chaotic. Their credibility comes largely from the battles they have fought and won. Power comes from performance.

The warrior figure is absolutely essential to the survival of the modern organization. Modern business is a battle, where the price of failure is defeat and death. Business needs its warriors.

❖

The basic task of heroes, on the other hand, is to discover the idea or insight that might regenerate the company, the category, the product, the service. Heroes know intuitively that the answer does not lie within the mainstream, with its prevailing attitudes, mindsets and beliefs. They realize that what now exists may be ineffective in the not-too-distant future.

What the hero must do is to withdraw from the mainstream and journey into what will feel like a wilderness because it is the new. The hero must visit the realm of uncharted experience. It is this journey that warrants the description heroic. In the modern organization this journey is, professionally and personally, dangerous. The likely outcome is that our modern-day corporate innovator will end up as a 'dead hero', with serious threats to career advancement.

Modern corporations are far more likely to reward their top warriors, than those who venture into places where there is no map, where there are no solid reassurances. The journey of the hero is a lonely one where the only motivating force is self-generated passion and belief. This is a poor currency in a culture that works on evidence, on fact. The work of the hero is, by and large, unrewarded. There is little chance of being granted immortality in an epic poem these days! The best the hero can hope for is a level of appreciation among a small core group within the organization who know his or her real value and courage.

To explore the hero and the heroic in this context is, I believe, to address the central issue in corporate life, namely, long-term survival and prosperity.

To survive, indeed thrive, in the long term, is the real challenge for a company, as it lives through the life cycle of a product, or through the maturing and ageing of a key category in which it competes. To survive and thrive, a company will have had to address, understand and integrate the hero. This is the individual or creative minority whose insights come from the journey away from the mainstream, whose task is to challenge the prevailing mindset, dogma and attitude, and whose vision is a new way of seeing the world.

THE WISDOM OF MYTH

To help us in our exploration we will avail of the authority and wisdom of the myths and legends of the world. We will draw from those stories that have truly survived the test of time.

The basic proposal is that the power of ancient myth can be harnessed to deliver results on major innovative tasks, which are critical to the future of today's businesses, large and small.

In seeking to benefit from the insights in this book, the reader will have a number of hurdles to cross. The first is a likely preconception about the word 'myth' itself. In ordinary parlance, 'myth' is synonymous with something that is untrue. We say 'that is a myth', when we talk of something that is false and to be disregarded.

Ancient myth conjures up that which is essentially untrue: stories that credulous peoples once accepted as literal fact, before the impact of modern science and rationalism swept away that belief. We are now tempted to regard mythology as having nothing to offer us but a view of ancient cultures very much removed from our own.

But to focus on the truth or falsity of a myth is to entirely miss its main point. Certainly, these stories were once taken as fact; and, of course, the modern consciousness refuses to accept those fabulous tales as true. However, the key question is not: 'Is the myth true?' but 'Is the myth useful?' And the argument of this book is that the ancient myths are as useful in our world as they were thousands of years ago.

What is a myth, if we disregard that irrelevant issue of whether it is true or not? A myth is a story, of a particular type and with a particular function. As stories, myths stand out because they are larger than life. They deal with great characters who have extraordinary adventures, in life-or-death situations.

Myths are exciting, racy tales but their original function was not merely to entertain simple communities gathered around the campfire after the sun went down, but rather to pass on a society's collective wisdom on what life was about: the origin of the world or of a particular community, the core values that underpinned the society, the principles that should govern behaviour either for individuals or groups. In a real, though not in a literal sense, myths told people what their world was like.

One particular myth, the myth of the hero's journey, is of particular relevance to those of us who are concerned with innovation. In fact it provides us with a well-spring of ancient wisdom on which we can draw. The myth of the hero's journey is remarkable in two respects. In the first place, it is a story that in one shape or form has recurred again and again across time and across cultures. Though the cast and the setting are different, the same basic theme recurs. Clearly, this myth is saying something which is of universal significance.

But even more remarkable from our point of view, the myth of the hero's journey addresses the central issues that must confront managers of innovation and change. This is because what the myth is essentially about is the challenge of the unknown.

It tells the story of the brave challenger who sets out from the comfortable setting of his homeground to venture into the unknown, an intimidating terrain where there are no ground rules or easy certainties, but instead one long series of trials and tribulations.

It spells out the nature of the obstacles he faces, and the imaginative way they are overcome. It reveals the great treasure that he eventually captures, but it stresses that the adventure is not yet over. The journey back to the homeground is as hazardous as the outward one, and the greatest obstacles may very well be those he meets on his return home.

No one who has been involved in the innovation process within major organizations can fail to be struck by the almost spooky similarities between the journey made by innovators and the hero's journey as set out in this universal myth.

Why is this useful, one may ask, this matching of a classic myth with the typical experience of a modern innovator?

Well, first of all, it provides the innovator with the shock of recognition. What had previously been unknown treacherous territory, a minefield with no indication of where its terrors lay, now becomes more familiar. The innovator can claim, I am not alone. My experience is not unique. Others have been there before me. Secondly, and more importantly, the myth provides a type of road map for the innovator, and, with map in hand, he or she can anticipate the kind of problems that are on the way. The map brings a measure of knowledge into a situation that up to now was often a succession of unpleasant surprises.

Of course, having a map does not in itself make the innovator's journey any easier. Change of any kind involves risk, with a downside matching every upside. But with a map for the journey, the innovator's confidence is increased, and with it the chance of eventual success. The innovator now has a clearer sense of what must be done, a clearer awareness that what may appear to be devastating setbacks are no more than stages on the way forward. However, having a map of this kind is not the same as buying a publication from the Ordnance Survey.

This book does not supply a neatly tabulated list of rules for innovation. It does not enable the executive to escape the risk and the uncomfortableness involved in innovation.

What, hopefully, it does provide is a totally new way of looking at the innovation process. Your view of what innovation is, and of the way it comes about, may be changed, and it is from that changed view that changes in action will flow.

THE PLAYERS IN THE KINGDOM

The picture of innovation offered to us by the myth of the hero's journey is one in which there are several players, all playing essential roles in the future of the kingdom.

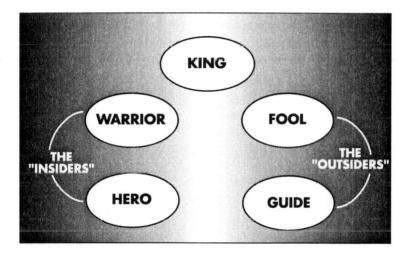

Fig. 1.1 The key players in the myth.

Apart from the hero who makes the journey, there are other players who do not necessarily leave the homeground. There is the king, there is the warrior, there is the fool, there is the guide. The myth tells us that each has a role to play in the story (see Fig. 1.1).

In the world of myth, the king rarely makes the journey. There are exceptions to this in mythic literature, but in many cases they are cautionary tales. The myth suggests that the first task of the king is to preserve his kingdom, and to preserve his power within it. If he goes on a hero's journey, he may find his kingdom seized from him, or decayed beyond repair, when he returns home. His task is to keep the kingdom in readiness for the great treasure that the hero brings back.

Nor is it usually the king's task, so the myth suggests, to choose the hero. The hero usually emerges. He may not be the 'ideal' choice, he may not be the person the human resources department would have selected. But he goes on the journey, while others don't, because he is driven by a stubborn vision or troubled by a nagging doubt. He goes because of who he is and what he is. ('He' is sometimes used, for convenience, and also as a reminder that these myths, for all the wisdom they have to offer us, are thoroughly sexist in presentation!)

The king's role in this is to let him go, to protect him to the extent he can, and to be ready to accept what he brings back. In indulging the hero, the king remembers that many years earlier he had also made the hero's journey. Perhaps he knows what the hero faces, even though he has now become a different person. The role of hero is not one for life. Rather is it something that certain people undertake at a particular stage of their lives. Making the hero's journey may indeed be itself part of another journey. To stay too long in the hero mode is to risk burnout and a diminishing record of success. The wise hero knows when it is time to move on.

The role of warrior is one of support for the king. Someone must defend the kingdom while the hero is away on his search. If the kingdom crumbles in the meantime, there will be no use for the treasure that the hero brings back. However, the great warriors are the preservers of the *kingdom*, not the preservers of the status quo. It is all too easy for warriors to see their role as defending the ways of the past against the new approaches that the hero has discovered. A more appropriate self-image for the warrior is as a defender of the kingdom's interest, whatever form that may take in changing circumstances.

The role of guide is an important one, though it does not provide the limelight that is the hero's due. The guide has knowledge that helps the hero along his way, but he or she does not make the journey himself. Indeed he cannot, despite his superior knowledge of the journey. Perhaps it is because his knowledge brings with it a detachment that would handicap a hero. Or perhaps it is because the best guides are often in some sense outsiders to the kingdom. Whatever the reason, the good guide knows the limits of his role and does not try to overstep them.

The fool, likewise, is an outsider, the one who against all the odds embodies truth, that piercing insight into reality which others refuse to acknowledge, but refuse at their peril.

Perhaps, uncomfortably, as you read this book, you see yourself cast in the role of one of the 'enemies' the hero meets along the way, the dragons and the demons that are part of every journey myth. If so, be reassured: these beings have their essential role, too. And it is well for the innovator to realize this, because it will help him to avoid feelings of personal animosity towards those who oppose him. The role of demons and dragons is to test the hero. Surviving such tests makes the hero truly heroic.

ROLES OF THE KEY PLAYERS

King
Preserves the kingdom and its power. Keeps the kingdom in readiness for the treasure to be brought home by the hero. Protects the hero

Warrior
Defends the kingdom while the hero is away. Preserver of the kingdom, but not of the status quo

Hero
Ventures into the unknown. Long service of trials and tribulations. Self-chosen in many cases. Has a stubborn vision or is troubled by a nagging doubt

Guide
Knowledge and wisdom to help the hero along the way. Cannot make the journey, but has access to the magical power the hero needs to equip himself with. May be an outsider or even an outcast

FRAMEWORK OF THE BOOK

The pattern of the book is straightforward. Chapter 2 sets down the story of the hero's journey. It provides short summaries of some of the major myths and brings together what is common from the many recurrences of this story across different cultures and different times.

Chapter 3 enters the modern world with two contemporary stories. These are actually a 'collage' of experiences drawn fictionally from a number of different companies and projects. The tales are specific and yet not unique to any particular company. One tale is based on the area of breakthrough innovation. The other is drawn from a typical culture change/total quality programme. They are contemporary stories of 'hero's journeys' in modern corporate life.

Chapter 4 focuses on the particular problem of 'the return journey' and draws a parallel with ancient myth in suggesting that companies, like ancient societies, tend to kill off their returning heroes. The 'dead hero' phenomenon is not a new one, as a study of the Greeks after the Trojan War will reveal. This book argues that proper re-integration of the hero figure is a central challenge for management. If initiatives for change are littered with 'dead heroes' then the organization has not only lost many of its best and most enthusiastic people but it has effectively destroyed its own future.

Chapter 5 looks at what the hero and the organization can do to help smooth the journey. Of course the path of innovation is never smooth, but this chapter argues that there is much that can be done, especially regarding the return journey, to significantly increase the probability of success. Among the tools which are analysed are road maps, the power of storytelling and certain symbols of transformation. This chapter also takes a close look at the characters the hero will have to encounter before, during and after the perilous journey. What about the warriors, the guardians, the king, the craftsman, for example, and what roles do the fool, the trickster and the fellow traveller play?

Chapter 6 focuses on actions the organization can take to help its heroes and ensure that it succeeds in real transformation. We look at ancient rituals and their close connection, throughout history, with myth and legend. We consider the rites of passage of the Greeks and the Celts to begin to define how a company might effect its own 'corporate rite of passage'. These explorations are then adapted to suggest a framework of initiatives that organizers of innovation and change can take to ensure good results and eliminate possible 'collateral damage' to its people and especially its hero figures.

Chapters 7 and 8 attempt to establish certain principles for managers of innovation and change. It is important that these principles are read in the context of the stories and experiences out of which they grew. This book is based on an inductive approach that seeks to draw out principles from real lived experience. It avoids the more common deductive approach that goes from theory or principle to the specific real-world application. We refer again briefly at this stage to the academic conventional wisdom on the subject of change.

Finally, in the Appendix, the book list will gear the reader towards further reading.

THEORETICAL CONTEXT

Possibly the most significant revolution in management thinking this century has occurred in the past 10 years. One word describes this change: process. The sophisticated manager in the 1990s is likely to be very sharp on 'process' in every sense of that term: supply chain process, innovation process, people process, change process, etc. Process consulting has developed as an important branch of business consultancy. The process revolution means a radical change in the way business is done.

This revolution offers a challenge to that cornerstone of management thinking, the hierarchy. The 'boss–subordinate' model of hierarchical management is being overtaken by the 'customer–supplier' concept.

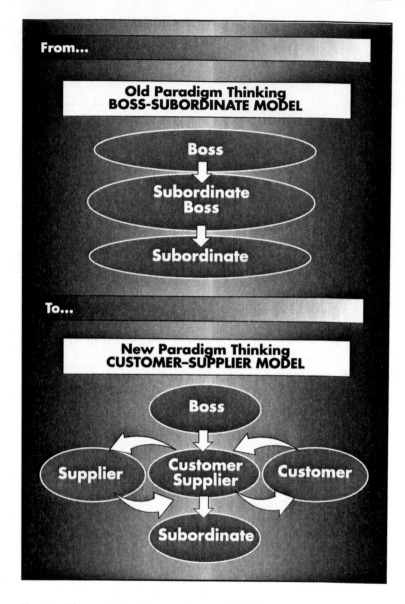

Fig. 1.2 The revolution in management thinking

Instead of managers defining their place in hierarchical terms of boss and subordinate, they are being asked to think of themselves as forming part of an interlinked set of customer–supplier relationships (see Fig. 1.2).

In fact modern-day managers are invariably called upon to initiate programmes to help bring about this very change. A revolutionary and busy time indeed, for managers.

This fundamental change is well documented in a number of recent books: W. Edwards Deming in *Quality, Productivity and Competitive Position*, J. M. Juran in *Leadership for Quality* and *Quality by Design*, Champy and Hammer on *Reengineering the Corporation*, Steven C. Wheelwright and Kim B. Clark in *Revolutionising Product Development*, Christopher A. Bartlett and Sumantra Ghosal in *Managing Across Borders* and finally Roussel, Saad and Erikson on *Third Generation R&D*.

These writers are leaders of the process revolution. They chart the subtle shift in emphasis from structure and system to the more dynamic world of 'how' organizations work. However, the focus of books by Deming or Juran of quality fame or by Champy and Hammer of reengineering fame is on the 'management of what exists', though with a process orientation. For many companies this has actually been a euphemistic way of cutting costs and re-structuring people out of the company.

The books by Wheelwright and Clark and the Arthur D. Little team are more focused on the management of what does not yet exist. Their subject is innovation and strategy through new product development and the management of research and development. They suggest the tools, techniques and processes which, they argue, will deliver the 'holy grail' of top-line growth through breakthrough innovation and breakthrough strategy.

The perspectives and tools proposed by these writers are very helpful. They tend to fail, however, to highlight the two most important ingredients in innovation: people and passion. First of all, it is people (of a very particular type) who are actually at the heart of successful innovation. And secondly, it is their passion for 'what does not yet exist' and about that which is not yet proven, tried and tested that is the energy at the heart of real success.

A company could follow every process, apply every tool, every technique in *Third Generation R&D* and *Revolutionising Product Development* and yet, without the people, deliver nothing. People of passion are a vital ingredient for a company which wishes to deliver real innovation. They are the magic ingredient. And they usually have a tough time in the modern corporation.

The theoretical focus of this book is that it is people (heroes) who actually make the difference through their entrepreneurial intuitive genius in the face of often adverse conditions.

The study of the hero is a well-trodden path. Homer, I would argue, was also essentially concerned with the dynamic of change, as were Virgil, Dante, Shakespeare, Milton, James Joyce and every great storyteller throughout human history. This book attempts to draw on the wisdom of some of these latter-day corporate advisers, but to go even further back and look at a vital source of inspiration of these literary greats: the rich world of myth and legend.

To do so will be to access an ancient wisdom that, I believe, will complement the insights of thinkers such as Deming, Kim Clark, Sumantra Ghosal and Philip Roussel. It provides a way of talking at some real depth about the people (in real companies) who are at the heart of these process-based change initiatives. Through the language of hero, warrior, king and guide, we are able to move back from the often distracting aspects of specific people and specific situations in actual companies and focus instead on the essentials of the roles people play in change initiatives. The task can thus be done in an affirming way – there are powerful positive connotations in being a hero, warrior, king or guide.

Mythology also provides a language to make explicit the forces and energies that are set in motion during every major change initiative. As already mentioned, these forces and energies are often more powerful than the systems and structures set in place to control them. They result from an inevitable resistance to new initiatives, the 'no change' agenda. The language and imagery of mythology, through concepts such as 'demons' and 'dragons', focusing on 'death and rebirth', enchantments (the story of the emperor's new clothes), fools, jesters and naivety, adds a very important theoretical (and indeed practical) contribution to the actual journey of change. It does so in a compelling and engaging way.

Finally, mythology has already been used very effectively to establish correlation in another vital area of change, the field of history. In his search for the underlying causes of the growth (and fall) of great civilizations, Professor Arnold Toynbee in his classic *A Study of History* rejects race and environment as the 'secret of success'. Instead he draws on Greek tragedy – the Promethean Trilogy of Aeschylus, and in particular the character of Prometheus – to highlight his central thesis, his belief as to why a civilization finally fails or survives.

Prometheus Bound is the one part of the trilogy left to us. It deals with the conflict between Zeus and Prometheus. Zeus has no wish other than to preserve his own position and the status quo. Prometheus, on the other hand, is the 'insatiable creator, a bringer of fire, a probing progressive mind'. Prometheus tries by rational means to convince Zeus that his universe is nothing but a desert, a wasteland. He fails. In time, he takes Zeus on, steals the fire and thus incurs the wrath of the vengeful king. In the contest he is physically at the mercy of Zeus and is tortured by the tyrant.

And yet, through sheer force of will, Prometheus is the victor. He guards a secret (of Zeus's demise), and through will-power wins out. According to Toynbee, this is at the heart of change. The secret is that, if Zeus persists in his static and tyrannical posture, he is dooming himself to be overthrown, like his predecessor, by the brute force which he has deliberately enthroned in the place of thought.

However, for a civilization (or surely a business) the solution lies in the reconciliation of Zeus and Prometheus. (Dramatically, it is believed this occurs in the two plays that are now lost to us.) Inevitable is the challenge (to Zeus) and inevitable is the response (initially wrathful). The hero Prometheus will be wounded by the thunderbolt of Zeus. The way forward is to move beyond the damage wrought by the initial challenge and response, towards accommodation.

If the vengeful response is inevitable (hero beware), the eventual accommodation is not. However, and this is the Toynbee thesis, the eventual decline of the civilization (or in our context, business) is inevitable if these two archetypal forces fail to 'do business'.

Prometheus Bound might be the basis for a modern management/leadership lecture. However, it was staged initially, not at the Harvard or Insead Business School, but at the Theatre of Dionysos in Athens in front of 15 000 people (including all the key politicians, military and business leaders of this day). It would have been part of a great community event – a festival of drama and comedy.

This staging of *Prometheus Bound* would have given a message to the great and powerful in early fifth-century Athens. The dramatic message being that it is important to take on Zeus (metaphor for the established order) and to do the equivalent of stealing the fire of the gods. Vengeance is inevitable but victory will come in the end.

We can only speculate now as to the effect of such a powerful dramatic message (or leadership lecture) being heard by really all the key figures of Athenian society, at the same time. The 'promethean' characters in the audience were being encouraged to take on the existing order. If this is speculation, what is not is the remarkable set of achievements of Athens at that time. Fifth-century Athens provided a 'benchmark' of excellence we still admire and imitate today. The dramatic festival would have provided the dynamism for such achievement.

Myth, then, was at the centre of fifth-century Athens. It was at the heart of Toynbee's thesis of great (and fallen) civilizations. It is still relevant today, relevant, that is, if our task is rebirth and the creation of what does not yet exist.

But let us leave myth and history for a moment, because the real authority that counts for most pragmatic business people is their own lived experience. To the extent that they are open to the insights of others, it will tend to be those others who have been visibly successful, over the long term.

This book does not, however, refer to the stories of the modern-day successful. It is hoped that the framework of myth and legend might help the reader articulate his or her own theory of innovation and change. The reader is invited on a journey into ancient myth and modern-day innovation. The actual territory travelled is not the battlefields of Troy or the grand visions of Milton or Dante, but the mundane experience of the modern office. Here, today, every day, are examples of the hero and the heroic. The stories in Chapter 3 are about everyday heroism. The task of the modern hero is to create the extraordinary from the ordinary, to find the 'jewel, elixir, boon' in the wasteland. It's tough, it always has been and always will be, but it can be done.

2

THE HERO'S JOURNEY

A Universal Story across Time and Cultures

O Saga of all that has happened
we know the tales and still
must we too be wanderers?
– Michael O'Siadhail

CONTENTS

- Introduction
- The First Stage: Preparation
- The Second Stage: Escape
- The Third Stage: Tests and Trials
- The Fourth Stage: Supreme Ordeal and Reward
- The Fifth Stage: Homecoming

INTRODUCTION

The hero's journey is invariably one which starts and ends in the same place: a familiar, secure territory that we shall call the homeground. This territory might not be as impressively protected as the city of Uruk was in the epic *Gilgamesh*, but it will always be a safe haven which its inhabitants are reluctant to leave.

The journey the hero undertakes is a perilous excursion from the safety of this homeground into the dangers and uncertainty of an uncharted world outside. There, in the unknown other world, the hero battles against massive obstacles to discover a treasure of critical importance to the people of the homeground.

After an equally perilous return journey, he often has to face the task of persuading his people to accept the value of the treasure he has won for them.

A universal element in the stories is that, to find the treasure, the hero must journey outside the walls of the homeground. The treasure can never be found within the protective walls of home. The hero must step out into the unknown; he must turn his back on safety and take on great risks.

What motivation underlines this journey of discovery? What is it that persuades the hero to turn his back on comfort and safety, and choose instead to put his life on the line?

THE ILIAD

The *Iliad* begins in the tenth year of the Trojan War, focusing on the crisis in the Greek camp, and the tragic circumstances of those involved in the conflict. This war was started to recover the 'face that launched 1000 ships' – Helen of Troy – who had been abducted by Paris.

The leader of the Greeks at Troy, Agamemnon, demands to take Briseis, the slave girl who was the war prize won by Achilles, the greatest warrior at Troy. Achilles withdraws, along with his men, from the battle until she is returned, causing much hardship to the Greek army. His mother persuades the king of the gods, Zeus, to give the Trojans the upper hand in the conflict, thus driving home to Agamemnon the pain caused by her son's absence. Zeus agrees and the Greeks suffer at the hands of the Trojans, led by Hector, the Prince of Troy.

So, frustrated by the circumstances surrounding the Greek force, Patroclus, Achilles' friend and colleague, asks to be allowed to enter battle. Achilles agrees reluctantly, but demands that his partner does not become too greedy with success. This is in the interests of Achilles' own personal conflict and the safety of Patroclus. While succeeding at first, Patroclus is eventually killed by Hector.

Achilles quickly agrees terms with his leader, and returns to the battlefield to avenge the killing of Patroclus. Hector and Achilles meet, and Achilles kills his adversary with a ferocious intensity. In his continuing rage he mistreats Hector's body refusing to return it for burial, until he is assuaged by Hector's father, King Priam. The *Iliad* ends with the funeral games of Hector, and despite its theme of war and conflict, fails to glorify the particulars of war. Instead it focuses upon the suffering on its participants, showing the tragic fates of both Achilles, whose death is foretold, and Hector, whose fate is symbolic of the future destruction of Troy.

In the universal myth, the journey often begins because there is an explicit threat to the homeground. A crisis calls into question the safety and the comfort of the homeground. Thus:

- the Eastern epic *Ramayana* begins when the Kingdom of Kosala is threatened by the tyranny of the wicked king Ravana.
- The epic *Beowulf* begins with the murders of Hrothgar's warriors by the gruesome monster Grendel.

In other stories, it is a theft or a loss of something of great value which puts the status quo in jeopardy:

- In the *Iliad,* the beautiful Helen was stolen.
- For the Chinese hero *Bao Chu,* the challenge is to recover the sun which had been stolen by the demon king, leaving the hero's village cold and dark, without trees, crops or flowers.

GILGAMESH

The text of the epic poem dealing with the Babylonian hero, Gilgamesh, is badly corrupted and much of the content is lost. However, the main facts remain. Gilgamesh is said to have been half human and half divine, and the ruler of the city of Uruk during the third millennium BC. The rule of Gilgamesh was oppressive and the god Anu decided to temper it by creating Enkindu as a softening influence. Enkindu came into being as a wild man, but he journeyed to Uruk where he acquired 'civilization' and met with Gilgamesh. The two became close friends and went forth upon many quests and adventures together which are described in the epic. At one point Gilgamesh rejected the marriage proposal of the goddess of love – Ishtar – and so in anger she sent a bull to destroy him. Enkindu helped his friend to defeat this bull, and together they killed it. The gods then decided that Enkindu was to die for this wrong, and the warrior subsequently fell ill and wasted away.

After his funeral, Gilgamesh journeyed throughout the land searching for Utnaphishtim, the sole survivor of the Babylonian Flood which created the world, in order to discover from him how to escape death, for Utnaphishtim was the only man who had this knowledge. Utnaphishtim showed Gilgamesh where to find a plant which supposedly renewed youth, but on his way back to Uruk, Gilgamesh had this plant stolen from him by a serpent. Yet the conclusion of the epic inexplicably tells of the return of Enkindu from the underworld with a report of what he found there and a promise to aid Gilgamesh in the recovery of the plant and various other items he had lost or had taken from him by the gods, the loss of which were affecting his happiness and status in the world.

Sometimes, the challenge comes from within the homeground rather than from outside. In the Arthurian legend, 'the Knights of the Round Table', the threat that Merlin recognizes and King Arthur addresses is the danger of civil war between the nobles, a danger that looks set to pull the kingdom apart.

If the first ingredient of the classic story is a threat to the security of the homeground, the second is a hero who will make the redeeming journey. *Who* is this hero?

Here again, as with the word 'myth' itself, we need to peel away from the term 'hero' the layers of misleading connotations that we might be tempted to attach to it. The hero of classical myth is by no means always a Hollywood-type hero. At first acquaintance, some of these heroes seem to be singularly lacking in what we have come to think of as 'heroic' qualities:

- Achilles is certainly a truly awesome warrior, but one whose petulance when thwarted could best be described as childish.

- The epic hero Gilgamesh is an arrogant, selfish young man, intensely disliked by his people because he oversteps his kingly rights in interfering with their lives.
- The hero knight in the *Parsifal* story is a totally naive, rather gauche, unsophisticated young man.

It is tempting to conclude that often these characters are not at all 'heroic' before they set out on their journey; rather the journey provides the opportunity for them to become heroic. The journey is part of their personal evolution. It is in the journey that they find themselves.

THE *ODYSSEY*

Homer's epic recounts the wanderings of the Greek hero Odysseus from the Trojan War back to his home in Ithaca. Since Odysseus' departure for Troy, his home had descended into anarchy and his city has been left without leadership. The king's return had been long awaited, but equally less certain. His son, Telemachus, embarks on a voyage to ascertain the whereabouts of his father.

Since his departure from Troy, Odysseus had travelled to numerous lands and had met with mixed fortunes. He encounters the ferocious Cyclops, speaks with the spirits of the Underworld, gives way to the lures of two female figures, Circe and Calypso, and is given plentiful hospitality by the Phaeacians, to whom he describes his adventures.

With their help he returns home, but using the assistance of friendly advice, he doesn't reveal his identity immediately. Instead Odysseus, disguised as a beggar, seeks sustenance at his own palace, only to be lambasted by the suitors who occupy his dwelling and hope to win the hand of his wife Penelope.

A competition to string and shoot Odysseus' bow was set, to decide the king's successor. Odysseus succeeds in being allowed to attempt the challenge (still disguised) and, to the horror of the suitors, accomplishes the task when all who tried previously had failed. A slaughter of the suitors follows by Odysseus and some colleagues whom he trusted with his true identity (including his son). The king is then reunited with his wife and father, but in the knowledge that his wanderings are not yet at an end.

But how then are these characters selected for the journey? How does a king know who to send, or how does a prospective hero know within himself that he is of the heroic mould?

Usually the king does not himself make the journey and when he does, there is serious danger that the kingdom will be neglected in his absence. Thus, the journeying king/hero *Odysseus* finds on his return that his palace has been overrun by suitors, who are not only feeding and drinking at his expense but are also seeking the hand of his wife Penelope and are intent on killing his son Telemechus.

So, if he does not go himself, how does the king make his choice of hero?

The myths sometimes, but only sometimes, mark out the hero with exceptional gifts or skills:

- Beowulf has 'the strength of 30 men in the grip of his hand'.
- Sigurd the Volsung is an obviously gifted young man, remarkable right from the time of his birth, both loved and admired for his size, strength, courage, intelligence and kindness.

SIGURD THE VOLSUNG

The Volsung Saga was the most popular tale of mortal heroes among the Norse myths and legends. The family line could be traced back to Odin – the leader of the gods – and each generation overcame great obstacles and performed wondrous deeds. Sigurd the Volsung was the son of Sigmund and the princess Hiordis, whom Sigmund married in his old age. He himself was ambushed and slain in battle when they were only newly married, but Hiordis was already pregnant. She was taken as wife by Elf the Viking who reared her son, Sigurd, as his own, and entrusted his upbringing to Regin – supposedly the wisest of men. Sigurd grew up to be a noble warrior and was a favourite of the god Odin. One day Regin told Sigurd the story of his own past which involved his being cheated out of a share of discovered treasure by his brother, Fafnir, who subsequently turned into a dragon who constantly guarded this treasure. Regin asked Sigurd to avenge this wrong and to this end fashioned him an invincible sword out of the fragments of the weapon previously worn by Sigmund and originally granted him by Odin. With the help of advice from this god, Sigurd slew the dragon and also Regin who plotted treachery against him. As he went on his way he heard of a maiden asleep on a mountain cliff, surrounded by a barrier of flames through which only the bravest of all men could pass. Sigurd was the first man to surmount this barrier successfully, and on the far side he found a sleeping figure encased in armour. When he removed this armour he saw a beautiful woman who fell in love with him the moment she awoke. She was Brunhild, one of the Valkyries who had been banished to earth for offending Odin. The two promised to marry and Sigurd gave her a gold ring as a token of his love. He then left her and went to the land of the Niblungs, where he was enchanted into forgetting Brunhild and marrying Gudren, the princess of that land, instead. Her new brother-in-law, Gunnar was encouraged to seek out the legendary Brunhild and win glory by passing through the fire for her. Still enchanted, Sigurd aided Gunnar on this quest and helped him to succeed. Brunhild was bitterly disappointed that it was not Sigurd who had come for her, but had no choice but to agree to marry Gunnar. When Sigurd saw her again at their marriage ceremony the enchantment was broken but there was nothing he could do. Out of grief and anger Brunhild asked Gunnar to kill Sigurd, which he did as the warrior lay sleeping in his bed. At the funeral Brunhild forgot her anger and, in grief, committed suicide, thus ending the section of the *Volsungen* saga dealing with Sigurd.

In other stories, it is one particular deed that suddenly reveals the heroic potential:

- King Arthur shows no signs of outstanding strength before he succeeds in pulling the sword Excalibur from the stone.
- Before Rama draws back King Janaka's right bow after the king's strongest warriors have failed to do so, he has dem-

onstrated no evidence of superior strength.

But sometimes, the hero may be very ordinary indeed, or conspicuously weaker than others around him:

- The point about Tom Thumb is that he is tiny.
- The central meaning of the David and Goliath story emerges from the fact that David is smaller and weaker than his opponent.
- Hans Castorp, Thomas Mann's heroic character in *The Magic Mountain*, is a patient in a sanatorium.
- James Joyce's Stephen Daedalus is naïve and inhibited from taking action.

These instances, in particular, tend to illustrate the fact that the hero's journey provides an opportunity of transformation for the character who makes it. He does not always come ready-made for the task.

THE FIRST STAGE: PREPARATION

The hero does not set out on his journey unprepared. He needs to be specially equipped, with specific skills, with specific tools or with the support of helpers to carry out specific roles:

- Sigurd the Volsung was taught many languages and other skills by his tutor Regin.
- Gilgamesh received from the gods the ability to learn from experience.

Sometimes the tools with which the hero is equipped are of a fantastical character, offering him protection that is not necessary in the comfort of the homeground but which is essential if he is to face the hazards of the unfriendly world outside:

- Beowulf is protected by a golden garment and an ancient helmet that no battle blade could bite through.
- Bao Chu in his quest for the sun is protected by a coat that miraculously prevented him from freezing.
- Gilgamesh had his metalsmiths build him an enormous bronze axe.

Though often the hero's journey is a solitary one, in some stories he is accompanied by a fellow traveller or an entire band of helpers. Gilgamesh stands out as a superb teambuilder. He recruits Enkidu after the two have battled together. They are helped not only by Shamash, the radiant god of the sun, but on a more mundane level by a team of 50 countrymen. Before he leaves, he wisely seeks advice from the elders of the city of Uruk, and while on the journey he seeks help as he needs it, for example, from the fishwife Sudwi and the scorpion man. *Beowulf*, too, carefully chooses a team of 14 brave warriors to accompany him on his quest.

BEOWULF

The Anglo-Saxon epic based around the deeds of the warrior Beowulf tells of how the royal house of Denmark, with King Hrothgar as its head, was being dishonoured and weakened by the nightly attacks of a monster known as Grendel. Each night this creature visited the royal household and carried off one of the king's men. Eventually, no warrior would remain in the great hall after dark. A noble from Sweden, Beowulf, heard of the Danish plight and sailed to their aid with 14 companions. He was welcomed by the king and once his worth as a warrior was proven through songs and tales of his previous deeds, Hrothgar entrusted the safety of his hall to him. Grendel visited the hall again that night and carried off one of Beowulf's men, but in a pitched battle Beowulf fatally wounded Grendel by tearing off his arm. The next day was given over to celebrations, but that night Grendel's mother visited the hall to avenge her son's death, and she carried off one of Hrothgar's most loyal retainers. Beowulf followed her to her lair in a swamp and after a mighty struggle defeated her with the help of a giant sword he found in her cave, since she shattered his own. He brought her head and the hilt of this sword back to Hrothgar's hall as trophies from this enounter. He sailed home enriched with treasure and ultimately became ruler of his own land, much beloved by his people until his tragic death in battle with a dragon who was ravaging the countryside. In this encounter Beowulf was deserted by all his followers, yet despite being mortally wounded himself, he defeated the dragon, and then died, leaving his people filled with remorse and sorrow.

In the *Ramayana*, the hero recruits a monkey to find out the whereabouts of the abducted Sita.

However, in some versions of the myth the hero sets out alone, even though he might get occasional help along the way. In the Holy Grail legends, for instance, it is mandatory for the hero to enter the forest alone. And even when accompanied, it becomes clear that the leader is set apart from his companions. He has special qualities of leadership, special qualities of vision.

The guide is a helper of a different kind. Wisdom is his essential characteristic. He is the one who knows the ways of the unfriendly outside world. He is often the one who has access to the mystic powers that the hero needs. The guide is often an outsider, perhaps even an outcast. And it is because of this separateness from the rest of the hero's world that the guide can offer insight of an altogether higher order.

The guide may be a magician, like Merlin or Gandalf, but while he has the gift of vision, he does not have the capacity to act: that is reserved to the hero. The guide can advise, but cannot make the journey himself. So while the hero relies heavily on the guide, in a crucial sense he remains superior to him. While the guide can point the way and help to prepare the hero, it is only the hero himself who can make the journey.

THE SECOND STAGE: ESCAPE

Suitably prepared, the hero is ready to embark on the journey. But first he must escape from the homeground itself. Often the way out to the world is guarded by a demon, a dragon or a monster. The terror of encountering such a creature is quite enough to prevent most people from even daring to venture outside the homeground. And as the stories tell us, this is an opponent who must be confronted and defeated. The hero cannot hope to slip by him. It is the first great challenge of the journey:

- Bellerophon has to kill the monster with three heads – the heads of a lion, a snake and a unicorn.
- St George has to confront the dragon breathing fire.
- Jason kills a dragon to win the Golden Fleece.

- Odysseus has to brave the one-eyed cyclops who is intent on eating him and all his men.

The hero must confront this guardian of the threshold and if he defeats the dragon, he will find something of immense value, something that he really needs on his journey.

- By drinking the blood of the dragon Fafnir, *Sigurd* is able to understand the language of the birds.
- Beowulf, having slain the giant Grendel, is rewarded by many gifts which will help him greatly on his journey.

In other cases, the payoff for slaying the guardian of the threshold is a treasure in the conventional sense: gold, jewels, goblets, coins. But it is clear that the most important reward is of a different kind.

The real significance of this first confrontation, and the reason why it cannot be avoided, is that in finding the courage to confront the guardian of the threshold the young man begins to become a hero. This is the first essential stage of his transformation. What has happened up to now was no more than preparation. Now the journey has truly begun.

THE THIRD STAGE: TEST AND TRIALS

With the threshold successfully passed, the hero is well and truly in a new world. The journey ahead of him is characterized by a bewildering series of tests, trials and obstacles. One effect of this process is that the hero may begin to lose grip on his own identity, often vacillating between overconfidence and despair.

It is in creating this stage of the journey that the mythmakers and storytellers are most in their element, giving free rein to the imagination. The mythic tradition has developed thousands of tests and trials of the most diverse kind, and in the telling of each challenge the myth has a clear message attached to it.

Some themes that recur across the worldwide history of myth include the following.

The series of tests

There seems to be a message in the frequency with which the hero is presented with a long succession of challenges, the 12 tasks of Heracles (Hercules in Roman myth) being a typical example. No sooner is one great challenge surmounted than another and yet another is encountered.

The mythmakers are telling us that a hero must be a person of remarkable tenacity, strength of mind and patience, for he will be tested again and again before the journey is over.

The impossible task

Many of the tasks facing the hero are impossible at first sight. A hero may be challenged to 'find me a man to drink all the wine in my cellar', then 'find me a man who can eat a mountain of bread in a day' and then 'find me a ship that can sail over land and sea'. Or like Daedalus and Icarus, a hero may be confronted with the necessity to fly to escape from the labyrinth.

Very often, what the myths tend to be highlighting for us here is the necessity to unravel paradoxes. What is seen to be impossible is not so when we change the framework of how we regard it.

Riddles and puzzles

Through their emphasis on challenges that involve the solving of riddles and puzzles, the myths tell us that it is often more important to be smart than to be strong. Alice in Lewis Carroll's story must find a door to fit the key she has in her possession. No brute strength, only the magic password, will let Ali Baba into the cave of treasures. In Tolkien's *Hobbit*, Gollum's puzzles must be answered, like the riddles of the Sphinx.

Distractions and temptations

Every hero's journey is littered with temptations to lure him away from the course he has set himself. The successful hero is the one who is steadfast enough to resist these temptations. Odysseus orders his men to tie him to the mast, to resist the allure of the Siren's song. Sigurd the Volsung succeeds in sleeping for three nights with Brunhild without embracing her.

No pain, no gain

The hero's progress through the obstacles is fraught and deadly. Odysseus on his journey loses every one of his comrades. Daedalus succeeds in flying away from the labyrinth, but Icarus does not survive. The myths are telling us that sacrifice is part of the price the hero has to pay for the successful completion of his journey.

Befriending the rejected or the ugly

One recurrent motif is the need for the hero to search in the most unlikely places. It is the frog who must be kissed if the princess is to find her prince. It is the toothless hag who turns out to be the font of wisdom.

Seeking among what has been rejected

Inside Pandora's box was every evil and disease known to man, ample reason for avoiding it, perhaps. Yet also locked inside that box was the great prize of 'hope'. The myth is telling us not to be too hasty in rejecting possible sources of solutions to the obstacles in our way.

Steering the middle ground

Again and again the myths suggest to us that to be successful in navigating the obstacles on his journey, the hero must avoid extremes. For instance, Odysseus learns how to navigate the awesome passage between the monster Scylla and the whirlpool Charybdis.

THE FOURTH STAGE: SUPREME ORDEAL AND REWARD

Very often when the hero is nearing the far point of his journey he is overcome by complete and utter despair. He feels that his world is falling apart, that all the journeying was in vain, that the effort was meaningless.

This is what we might call 'the dark night of the adventurer'. It is the final stage that must be passed through. This is where the hero comes closest to death. Sometimes, he catches a glimpse of afterlife, through a visit to Hades, the underworld, the place of lost souls. In other stories, the climax of the journey is portrayed by a last encounter with a fearsome monster or with the forces of nature.

But if the hero passes through this supreme ordeal, survives the shipwreck or the thunderbolt, defeats the last dragon, or successfully navigates the waters of the Styx, then, at last, the time has come for him to discover the reward that he has sought.

Beyond this last dark night is a peaceful time and a peaceful place. Here the hero will encounter what it is he came to find, and here the meaning of his journey will suddenly become clear.

The reward is now his. The treasure that will secure the future of his kingdom, the valued possession or person that had been snatched away, whatever it was that the hero sought is now within his possession.

The elixir is his. But the journey is not yet over.

THE FIFTH STAGE: HOMECOMING

The story does not end there, because the myths have much to tell us about the perils of the return journey and the return to the homeground itself. Very often, the reward itself is fragile, and can be easily lost or damaged on the return. The hero needs not only to protect the treasure, but to make it most robust.

The danger is not only to the treasure. Many heroes, the myths warn us, do not make it back at all, or do not survive their return:

- Bao Chu does deliver the sun, but dies in his battle with the king of evil.

- Sigurd is killed by Gunnar, the victim of Brunhild's treachery.
- Beowulf dies in his battle with the fire dragon that threatens his kingdom.

One message the myths seem to be offering is that the hero should not accept too much by way of personal reward. He will deliver the elixir, but may not survive to enjoy the benefits it brings to his kingdom. There is no guarantee of 'happy ever after' for the hero.

For one thing, the hero is reminded that when he returns to the homeground he is once again bound by rules. He must be prepared to lose the wide degree of freedom that he enjoyed while on his journey. This is often symbolized by arcane conditions which the hero ignores at his peril:

- For Orpheus, it is the clear instruction not to look back. He fails to follow this instruction, and loses the reward, his wife, Eurydice, as a result.
- The Irish hero Oisín, on his return from the land of eternal youth, forgets the condition of return and puts his foot on the ground. Instantly, he is transformed into an old man and dies.

According to the myths, then, certain conditions apply to the way the hero must behave on his return to the homeground. The myths emphasize that the hero is returning to what has become, in a sense, a strange place for him. Time has passed, people have changed, and, above all, the people in the homeground have not shared the experience of his journey.

So he will often meet suspicion and hostility from those who stayed behind. Sometimes the kingdom will send out an emissary to meet him before he reaches the homeground, an emissary who may prove to be as formidable an adversary as the guardian of the threshold he had to confront on the way out. The emissary may often be more concerned with the continuance of the status quo than with the potential for improving the kingdom that is offered by the reward the hero is bringing back.

Some heroes *do* make it back, with both their lives and the reward intact. Some heroes are accepted, welcomed and indeed celebrated in the homeground. But, the myths make it clear, *none of this can be taken for granted.*

3

CONTEMPORARY HEROIC TALES

Some Stories from Modern Business

Gilgamesh strikes out for glory,
journeying to the Land of Cedars
to fight the giant Humbaba.
– Michael O'Siadhail

CONTENTS

- Introduction
- Taking Your Own Heroic Journey
- Frank Price's Journey into Innovation
- Jane Lipman's Journey into Culture Change

INTRODUCTION

In the quick glance we have taken at the universal hero's journey myth, you may already have seen connections with the business world in which you work. In this chapter we will make some of these connections more explicit.

We will make these connections in two ways. First, we invite you to follow the map of the Hero Journey in relation to your own life. The twelve stages are interspersed throughout the text and summed up in the diagram at the end of the chapter. You are guided with questions as to appropriate connections and reflections. Second we will tell two stories. These are stories that are true to life though they are not drawn from life. The two heroes we are about to meet do not exist, but aspects of them exist in many executives. In an important sense, he and she could be you.

As you read, you will get a feel for what it is like to use the road map of the hero's journey as a guide in the real world of today.

The first story concerns a high-flying executive named Frank Price. His task is to create a rebirth in the commercial fortunes of a multinational whose business is that of helping to wash a large share of the world's clothes. Frank's task is to enter into the territory of branded consumer goods in a mature, well-established field and somehow find something new, exciting and relevant.

This task is crucial to the company since market position and momentum have been slipping. Market dominance is crucial. It brings with it the profits and cashflow needed to fund investment in further research and advertising. Gaining or losing market share points is worth millions on the bottom line.

Our second story concerns Jane Lipman. Her task in itself is less critically strategic in that the fortunes of Fifth Wave, the company in which she works, will not rise or fall whether she succeeds or fails. Jane's project is one of 10 that have been set up in an attempt to fundamentally change the culture of a small computer technology company.

The future success of the company is dependent on people like Jane taking on much more responsibility and leadership. The programme is the vehicle of change. Jane Lipman is a vital part of its success.

TAKING YOUR OWN HEROIC JOURNEY

You may wish to use the narrative tales of this chapter to reflect on the Heroic Journey in your own life. This could be in your past, your future or, indeed, you might be in the middle of a Journey right now. As you will see as you work through the reflection, the Heroic Journey is broken down into twelve stages. You are invited to trace your own path – following and being guided by the ancient, yet contemporary, mythical map. Note that this Journey starts at Stage Two, for reasons that will be explained. The twelve stages are summarized diagrammatically at the end of this chapter.

FRANK PRICE'S JOURNEY INTO INNOVATION

Fabric washing is a market that Frank knows well: for years he has been in top-line positions within the division in several countries across the world. Frank has done well in meeting the challenges he has been presented with so far.

But here is a challenge of a different kind.

For one thing, Frank immediately recognizes, it is a challenge that won't be resolved merely by doing what has always been done. It won't be resolved, he feels, by the kind of small incremental improvements that have become the norm in the organization for many years. He knows that inching forward can be important. But he also worries that such an approach focuses on existing opportunities, not on finding new ones.

He worries that this kind of incremental 'innovation' is delivering less and less each year in terms of competitive edge. He worries even more that when the tide goes out on today's idea, the business may be left stranded on the beach because it has not built up a strong position to meet the challenging world of tomorrow.

After his years in the organization as a successful high-flyer, Frank has learned the safe way to handle his position. He knows how to approach it professionally, logically, so that he will look all right (and maybe even great) when the very senior people come around. He knows how to put in place a programme of action that will at least keep the defences strong and cut to a minimum any loss of market share.

STAGE TWO: THE CALL TO ADVENTURE

The Heroic Journey will typically begin with a 'Call to Adventure' or what the late great mythologist Campbell called the 'Twinkle Twinkle' syndrome. Note that we have started your journey at Stage Two to remind you that the journey won't necessarily start at the beginning, at the right time, at a time you are ready. It could start or have started anytime. But it does typically begin with 'the Call' (Stage Two) and the hero must then return to Homeground to deal with some issues (Stage One).

– *Reflect now on your own 'Call to Adventure':*

- It could be an inner voice calling at a time of quiet reflection.
- It could be a chance encounter on a plane or a train with a stranger who somehow inspires, intrigues, enchants
- It could be some words from a lecture, a presentation, a book or magazine that somehow say 'come with me'.
- It could be you are standing on a burning platform and have to advance.

– *How will you know your 'Call'?*

- It will be obvious because of the simultaneous feelings of excitement and fear
- The 'voice' that calls will keep coming back to mind

You will know that whether you respond or not, your life will never be the same again. You have had the 'call'.

One way of approaching Frank's job was presented in a discussion with a consultant friend of his. The wise, career-minded innovation manager, his friend proposed, starts a process of new product idea generation afresh and makes absolutely sure the timing is such that nothing effectively gets launched during his tenure in new product development (NPD). After all, the argument went, with 1 success in 10 for new launches, who wants to have that on his CV? Beware innovation jobs, was the advice; they can seriously damage one's career.

The consultant friend knew well that such politically astute but cynical behaviour was not in Frank's nature. If Frank had a fault, his friend thought, it was that he was too open and honest for large corporate life.

Frank Price was going to have a go at the challenge. He knew that the market-place tweaking of the established brands was not the answer at all. The real issue, he realized, was that the company had lost its ability to be truly creative. His job specification, his *mission*, was no less than to restore his organization's capacity to generate new ideas, to change in a fundamental way.

And while his choice was clear, Frank experienced the inevitable doubts that made him hesitate. He had a young family that was very important to him. His wife Cathy had a demanding job. Could he take on a task that he knew would require a commitment way beyond the call of duty? Did he want to face the loneliness involved, the uncertainty that would dog his every step? Was he ready to make sacrifices, in the knowledge that even if he succeeded in finding a breakthrough his efforts would not necessarily be appreciated (or rewarded) within the rigidities of the organization?

The 'no' voices in his head were explicit and clear. The 'yes' voices, in contrast, were vague and abstract. He talked it over with Cathy and she promised to support him in whatever he decided. No easy way out there. In the end he decided 'yes', but for no reason that he could easily spell out. Probably it was because he felt he could not live with himself easily if he chose the 'no' option.

STAGE ONE: HOMEGROUND

The Hero then must return to Homeground for there is business to be done. Metaphorically we can portray the Homeground as a box (boxed in) or a square or, perhaps, like in Tolkien's book *The Hobbit* where Bilbo's home is presented as everyone's favourite country cottage (garden, quaint, homely, fire etc.).

- *Reflect now on all those things you know and love in your life, your home, your work. You might like to list the things that keep you safe and reassured, be they things (diaries, computers, phones) or less tangible (attitudes, beliefs).*
- *Reflect too on the deep ambivalence you have to responding to the 'Call to Adventure'. Note the 'Yes' voices and all the reasons you want to go but also note the 'No' voices and all those reasons to stay right where you are.*

- *Holding both 'Yes' and 'No', see if you can find within a deeper place of choice that makes a clear decision to act on the 'Call to Adventure'.*
- *Make some plans to safeguard any things in your Homeground that you want to ensure are still around when you return.*

Having decided, Frank now had to prepare himself for his journey. Where, indeed, was he planning to go?

Instinctively he knew that a hectic 'fact-finding' world tour, a losing of himself in a whirl of activity, would provide no answers. He had already learned all he could from going out into the field and stirring up dust.

Frank realized that what lay ahead of him was essentially a journey of the mind, a thinking journey. And he realized that he was the one who must do the thinking, he was the one who must do the exploration. This was not the time to commission a consultant's report. As with the fact-finding tour, Frank realized that such a report would not provide the essential solution. He knew that the dynamism must come from within the organization. He had first to make the journey and then somehow persuade his colleagues to make the same exploration for themselves.

The immediate challenge though was to find the breakthrough necessary to begin his journey. He was searching for something that didn't yet exist. But where to start? How to start? What to actually do? Getting out of the box, out of the existing mindset, seemed an insurmountable problem. Frank suddenly felt a surge of sympathy for a US Director of Patents, one Mr Duell, who announced in 1900 that everything that could be invented already had been!

He looked around at the vast open-plan office that was one of the hallmarks of the company. Every member of staff, at whatever level, worked in an open office. This was very much the style of the company founders who had no time for corporate status symbols. Story had it that one of the founders had even been turned away by a security guard when he had left his identity card behind in a hotel room.

This open plan, where a new recruit could sit at a desk with the same specification as a board member was, in fact, no longer a good place for new ideas. There was enough 'energy' in that office to light a small town but it was no place in which to be exploratory or tentative or to make mistakes.

All Frank knew was that he had to get away from the office, simply to think.

WITHDRAWAL

One option that is always available in corporate life is to hire a consultancy. Frank felt this was particularly inappropriate in this case. Here was a task of discovery, a moving into the unknown. So, by definition, the agency surely would be as lost as he was. However, he did use a process consultancy which was into creativity. He know it as brainstorming.

The notion of brainstorming sessions presented itself as a possibility to him and Frank had been an enthusiast of this method. Now, however, it seemed to him that such sessions would only generate half-baked ideas that somehow would not survive the cold light of day. Lots of fun and enthusiasm, lots of flip chart paper. But then what?

He recalled one small group syndicate within one such a brainstorming session, a motley crew including a few rather strange characters from an outside agency. This group, after a slow start, had suddenly burst into creativity. Ideas flowed. They practically re-invented the company. The excitement was tangible. It had all made so much sense. The group had seemed to enter an almost 'trance-like' state, a state in which everything was possible, the world was abundant, normal boundaries and rules did not apply and it was somehow funny and serious, superficial and profound at the same time.

As Frank recalled this experience, he remembered how he had returned to the real (normal) world full of enthusiasm and passion, both for the approach and for the thinking it had achieved.

It was a painful experience. His colleagues had not the slightest interest in the approach. In fact some of the methodology of brainstorming seemed rather silly and trivial. What had been so real, just didn't seem the same in the cold light of day. The conference turned them down.

Frank needed to 'de-bundle' this experience and rescue now what was worth saving. The painful experience had caused him to dismiss it all, and this included the obviously valuable methods and techniques they had been encouraged to use.

Yes, he did want to re-enter that creative 'trance' again and to do it within a group. It would be a withdrawal from the 'normal' world to a place where all things are possible, where you visit what the Irish call 'Tir na nóg', the land of eternal youth. He wanted to find again that place of abundance and growth.

STAGE THREE: MEETING THE GUIDE

In many mythic journeys, the Guide(s) will mysteriously appear for the hero as they fully, consciously commit to the Journey. The Guide may travel together with hero or may simply offer once-off advice. Guides can be human, or even from the animal or natural world. To use non-human guides, Hero develops a 'Heroic Pose' which is a state of mind from which everything speaks. Hero learns from all aspects of the world.

– *Be prepared for strong challenges from those around you as you set off on the Heroic Quest. Friends, family, colleagues like you as they are and a collective cry will likely go up – 'Get back in Your Homeground'.*
– *The Guide that you need will appear when you are ready. Your task is to formulate the questions, hypotheses for your journey and not to search for a Guide.*
– *Develop clarity on your questions (what do I seek? what do I want/ need/desire?) and develop compelling hypotheses as to the right way forward (they will be wrong but start hypothesizing).*
– *Be open to a gift from the Guide be it a phrase/mantra or a little symbolic talisman that helps keep you together during later trials and tribulations.*

It was then that he decided to attend a creative thinking course. The course brought back some memories of the brainstorming session. There were moments when he felt the same trance-like effect where everything flowed in abundance. He also observed the effect one cynical mind could have on a group. Those flow moments came only when they split up into smaller groups, without the cynic. So, was creative thinking the way forward?

Well, yes and no. Frank sometimes had an incongruous picture of grown adults playing games. And yet he recalled something he'd learned in his schooldays, through the work of the famous Shakespeare critic A. C. Bradley and specifically Bradley on Hamlet. He remembered Bradley's first hypothesis interpreting the play. Frank thought, 'Brilliant! I now understand Hamlet!' But then Bradley demolished that hypothesis to put up another, a second hypothesis. 'I now *really* understand Hamlet', Frank felt. But again Bradley demolished it. By the time hypothesis three was constructed, a very important change had happened for Frank. He wasn't going to fall for it yet again, though for the life of him he couldn't see anything wrong with hypothesis three. It was really brilliant!

He had learned two things: the power of holding hypotheses and simultaneously detaching, letting go, to move beyond each hypothesis. The creative thinking course built on this process. One of the 'exercises' involved generating nonsensical ideas. He watched as even these 'crazy' starting points evolved, through the use of development techniques, into something practical, yet vital, new and exciting.

Through the creative thinking course, Frank re-experienced not *what* to think but *how* to think. In addition he picked up some tips on who to think with. He gained insight into creative flow in a group: it just seemed to happen with some people but was almost impossible with others. He began to develop a sense of who he could 'flow with'. He needed to re-enter that creative 'trance'.

Frank had a way now of mentally 'leaving the homeground', or at least a way of starting the journey. It was not a physical, but rather a mental leave-taking. It involved getting away from the thinking which the homeground encouraged, from the research reports, the analysis, the pervading mindset.

Frank was now mentally prepared for the journey. At least he thought so. But as he started to compose his thinking team, he realized he had a very serious challenge. He needed research scientists to think with. They were absolutely essential to his team. Alas, Frank realized that he would have serious problems getting them on his side, because there guarding the entrance to R&D was his first dragon, breathing fire all the way, the Head of Technology and Development, Geoff Stiles!

Geoff was good, excellent in fact, at delivering what the organization asked for. But he always operated within the framework of what was already there. Geoff, in Frank's eyes, was a past master at the art of tiny, incremental improvements, and a declared enemy of any approach that would take the organization in the direction of the radically new. His contempt for anything 'off the wall' had withered many a young researcher, had successfully wiped out the enthusiasm of many a new brand manager.

Strange, but true: that part of the organization which should be the fountain of change was actually most set against it. At least, Geoff was. Frank's big problem was how to deal with Geoff. He contemplated the option of totally circumventing the daunting head. Geoff after all, was going to be away for the whole of March. That opportunity tempted Frank. But knowing Geoff as he did, and remembering past encounters with him, Frank knew that circumventing Geoff was not the way. That strategy would catch up with him later. Geoff would get his own back, in spades. And Geoff was as tough as they came.

STAGE FOUR: CONFRONTING THE DRAGONS

Before the Hero can cross the 'Threshold of Adventure' into truly new ground, into that which has yet to be experienced, it is vital to confront the Dragon or Demons. This character, which is so beautifully portrayed in the myth, may be the Dragon in our head if we look at myths psychologically or it may be that colleague, friend, family member who somehow keep us 'stuck'.

- *Before confronting the Dragon/Demon, it is vital to make explicit the qualities of Hero within. What are all your heroic strengths and qualities? You will need them all and more.*
- *We know the Dragon/Demon through experience in life. Whenever we say 'if only Mr. X/Mrs. X weren't there, I could succeed....' He or she is your boss, your colleague, your partner, your lover. They somehow look, paralyse, castrate.*
- *Another Demon is the 'Demon Should'. This is all those internalized, learned 'should' voices which we have swallowed from family, society, friends. The Hero must confront the Demon Should to find that place where they 'want' to travel on, not they 'should' travel on.*

Frank felt powerless. He had met the Guardian at the threshold of the outer world and, despite all his preparation, he did not know what to do. He spent a lot of energy railing against Geoff to Cathy and to an artist friend and mentor, Jack Harris. Frank burned with frustration against Geoff himself, against the organization for sustaining Geoff in such a key position, against himself for being tripped up so early on the journey.

Then one evening, when Frank was complaining to Jack for the ninth time about the situation in which he found himself, Jack let slip a casual remark that helped Frank to move forward. 'We all get the enemies we are able for', Jack said. Suddenly, Frank saw the situation in a new light. Instead of fury and impotence, he began to size up Geoff as an enemy he could win over. He, too, had to fight, not necessarily to defeat Geoff, but certainly to get his way.

Spurred on by this new-found confidence and perspective, Frank began to think more coolly about Geoff. He attempted to see things from Geoff's perspective. With impotence and anger no longer blinding his judgement, he remembered a conversation he had with Geoff a long time earlier. Geoff had then maintained that he was not negative just for the sake of being so. He was critical, highly critical, because he believed that was the way ideas were purified, became clearer. He held that if ideas withered under the heat of his fiery first reaction, they were worthless. The good ideas, on the other hand, were the ones which survived that kind of treatment. When promoters of products came back with modifications that met Geoff's criticisms, then he was supportive. Or so he claimed.

Frank was immensely cheered-up by this recollection. If Geoff really believed this, then he felt his task was easier. Frank no longer had to convince someone who was set against change. He only had to convince Geoff that some kinds of ideas, the ones that involve enormous change, are too fragile to be exposed right away to the heat of criticism. He would have to persuade Geoff to hold his fire until a later stage and just to give him a little space. It was just as well, perhaps, that Geoff was away for a month, because it took Frank a long time to come to terms with this notion. Firstly, he had to convince himself that he could stand up successfully to Geoff, and secondly, find a means of doing it.

The enemy (dragon or demon) often holds something of great value. It's not smart to kill the dragon, Frank's friend Jack pointed out; it's not smart to ignore him either. Furthermore, the dragon is probably as much in one's own head, as out there. It was good advice. It had helped Frank to remove a significant mental block, and forge ahead with courage.

When Geoff returned from his trip, a newly confident Frank was waiting. Instead of the kind of pointless confrontation they usually had in the past, their meeting was calm. And to Frank's surprise, Geoff agreed readily enough to Frank exploring his hypothesis with a cross-section of the research resources at all levels. His one precondition was that he be continually updated on developments. The next stage of the journey could begin.

HOMEGROUND

Now, where do you go to get a breakthrough in products to wash clothes? Well, there are washing powders and, increasingly, washing liquids. And the basic thing a consumer wants, Frank realized, is obvious. It is a wash that works first time on all kinds of stain and dirt and that takes less of his or her time. Consumer studies also told him it was all about performance of the product, with convenience scoring second but a long way back. More recently environmental issues were getting a look in. The 'holy grail', of course, was that someone would invent a product that meant perfect cleaning and no ironing.

The basic 'tried and tested' approach to commercial success had been one of inventing a better chemical, bleach, enzyme, water softener so that a test against a competitor's product showed a visible result. Then over to the marketing people to advertise the victory. All one needed was the scientific know-how to invent better chemicals. Quite simple really! Just follow the formula!

The only problem was that victories in consumer product dem-onstration had been reduced to showing a victory over the competitor when spaghetti sauce was spilled over a white shirt. Yes, my enzyme was better than yours in removing spaghetti sauce. So what! Consumers, in the meantime, were becoming increasingly sceptical. They were fed up with the better, better, better and whiter, whiter, whiter advertising of the industry. They were also tired of the patronising way in which the prod-ucts were advertised.

Frank had to find a better way, a whole new way. Here was the corporate mindset he had to break. Somehow.

But how?

TESTS AND TRIALS

Frank's approach at this stage was to craft a series of events with diverse, almost random groups of people. The challenge confronting him was to persuade the right kind of people (open-minded, exploratory types) to join him on the journey. He wanted to enter that creative 'trance' with a chosen group and to do it a number of times.

His colleague Katie Brown helped him in his task. As well as being steeped in the technique and method of creative thinking, Katie had the ability to 'craft an emotional climate' where people felt safe. She became Frank's great support. She helped him form the emotional space for the journey every time a group got together. It wasn't a formula. It didn't always work. It was more a case of putting the ingredients (especially the right people) together and hoping for the flow, the group trance.

Frank had the further task of persuading the scientists to join in. A number of the really good people had had negative experiences of previous innovation initiatives. Some of them had felt 'used', to put it bluntly. He had to win their trust again. Frank was actually very good with people, and after a while the scientists did open up. This led on to yet another challenge. They spoke of their passion for science and learning and for Frank it was a matter of holding his own in conversations about quantum mechanics and NMR spectroscopy and tectonic and thermal process in the lithosphere, digital telecommunications and electronics and microbiology. As he penetrated into the belly of the scientific whale, he also found himself talking about Shiva and Hindu mythology, and trade union politics, and Yeats's poetry, and good restaurants in Chile, and the psychology of ageing, and Roland Barthes and de Saussure and semiotics, and the meaning of Miss Piggy and the Muppets, and flora and fauna of the Orkneys, and Joseph Heller's *Catch 22*.

STAGE FIVE: TESTS, TRIALS, ALLIES AND ENEMIES

The confrontation of Hero and Dragon must end in accommodation for the Hero finds that the Demon/Dragon was not so bad after all. The Demon (within) was perhaps protecting something of great value to the Hero. And the Hero (within) was also not quite so heroic. The Hero/Dragon alliance is a strong place from which to tackle the tests and trials that lie ahead.

– *Most of all the Hero must actively seek out new experience to help get out of outdated ways of thinking. Make a list of new,* exciting adventures, people, events and go out and experience a few of them.

- The myths also advise attending to those things that are neglected, rejected, denied. You have to 'kiss a lot of frogs' before one will turn into a 'prince'. Take time out to be with the marginalized, scapegoated, the 'has-beens', the minority. They will probably offer a new angle on the world.
- The test and trial stage of the Journey will also pose inner challenges. A heroic journey will stretch you personally as well as professionally. Be prepared for the inner tests and trials. Some heroes use journals to reflect.

One thing he knew for sure. If he showed no interest in what they were passionate about, they would show no interest in his current passion – a breakthrough idea.

But actually, every journey into the passions of the scientists was somehow relevant. The creativity course had taught him the power of 'connection-making'. He was beginning to refine and develop his own hypotheses.

And along the way, Roland Barthes and semiotics had given him a whole new way of looking at advertising, trade union politics had raised his awareness about the politics of innovation and the challenges he would face later, and the Hindu god Shiva taught him the value of chaos and the relationship between creation and destruction. All good stuff, but only indirectly related to the primary task.

He also explored volumes of market research data. The challenge here was to avoid drowning in data. It was like one of those impossible challenges in fairy tales. Find three straws of gold in a barn full of straw. Nearly all of the material is waste. It is history, not the future. A quote from the creativity course kept coming to mind:

Discovery consists of seeing what everyone else has seen and thinking what no one else has thought.

It was from one Albert Szent-Györgi. It was a nice idea, but Frank still felt he drowned in the data. It left him feeling depressed.

By other routes, Frank (and his growing network) were developing a number of hypotheses in relation to the washing product:

- He was thinking of storage bags impregnated with detergent that one just throws into the washing machine full of socks or underwear. By working on clothes through a chemical in the bag, these would deliver a real convenience and performance benefit.
- He was thinking of a pill that slowly released the appropriate chemicals at different stages of the wash cycle. Again, this would deliver performance and convenience benefits.
- He was thinking of a mix-and-match box: all the ingredients would be separated and one effectively made up a wash powder depending on the kind of wash one had. This would deliver on performance (a better wash) and also on the environmental need to use fewer chemicals. There would be convenience problems, however.

These were just a few starting hypotheses. There were many more. Each creative event yielded its rich collection of ideas and insights. And what's more, an informal network had begun to grow around Frank's project. People were putting themselves out, sending him E-mail:s, prototypes, newspaper cuttings.

DISCOVERY

This journey, Frank was learning, was one of intense excitement and passion. The people he had attracted to his network were, without fail, passionate people, even if their passions ranged from the Queen of South Football team to packaging machinery. Together, they had become passionate about the journey and the hypotheses that were leading it. Passion was crucial because this is what drives an idea or a hypothesis. There is no track record, there are no facts, no loyal consumers, no corporate strategies. There is only one's own belief in something that exists in one's head, but not yet in the world. And somehow, with particular people, that new hypothesis grows, develops a life of its own and seems like it is the promised land. This is so exciting.

But if the journey is about passion, it is also about despair. Total despair.

STAGE SIX: APPROACHING THE INMOST CAVE (SUPREME ORDEAL)

The Heroic Quest will invariable include a time where Hero feels as if their world is 'falling apart'. This stage we can also call the 'Supreme Ordeal' or the 'Dark Night of the Innovator'. It will be recognizable when you wake in the middle of the night in a state of total disarray wondering why did you ever start and what is it all about. The Hero is a long way from Homeground with little to show for it but grief (and, of course, new experience).

- It is not possible to do much about the Supreme Ordeal but recognize it and acknowledge. It is something to live through. To fall apart, to die (not literally) to the past may be the best thing that ever happened. But it hurts.
- What can be done is to re-run all the valuable bits of the journey to date. Re-visit all the insights, learning, ideas and problems overcome for often insight will come from a reconfiguring of the past in a wholly new form.

The idea of a storage bag which in the washing machine released detergent and led to a better, more convenient wash started to fall apart as a way forward. The technical people could deliver a useful chemical pre-wash but there was no way of the bag doing it all. The powder or liquid was still needed. So the concept of 'wash bags' was beginning to look like a niche idea for the pre-wash stage. Nice idea, but commercially very small.

The slow-release pill solution that delivered different chemicals at various stages of the wash also began to fall apart. The washing machine was too turbulent and the wash pill would simply disintegrate, leaving blobs of coagulated chemicals poorly spread. Perhaps in 10 years the scientists told him, but not in the immediate future. The team had spent weeks exploring the technology of the large drug companies. But the inside of the body, where controlled release is possible, is very different from the inside of a washing machine.

And the mix-and-match solution proved from early consumer research to suit about 3% of consumers in certain parts of Germany with a passion for environmental issues and an upper-middle-class life style. But mix and match was simply not mainstream.

Frank was in despair. It felt like his whole world had fallen apart. In a three-day spell all the good creative work of months just seemed to disintegrate. One needs to go on a journey into innovation to really know that despair (or excitement). Very few of Frank's mainstream colleagues (not his innovation team) knew that place. They kept going on with their essential tasks running the day-to-day affairs of the business. But they knew nothing of this discovery, and none of this despair. They never tried to do anything really new.

There was also a total loss of momentum. Fellow travellers wondered whether they'd backed a loser. The excitement and passion of the journey felt like putting on wet clothes. Ugh! The group 'trance' of the creative workshop seemed more like collecting lemming-like madness than a re-invention of the world. In short, the whole thing was rather embarrassing. And how much easier never to have started.

It was perhaps what the mystics call the 'dark night of the soul', applied to the journey of innovation, a time when all that seems left is to let out a cry for help.

Frank felt stuck, stuck in a hole with a set of disintegrating hypotheses. All a very far cry from the initial grand intentions of rescuing the sinking ship. He felt like Icarus, flying too close to the sun and hurtling helplessly to the ground. Desperate. Very alone.

But then one night (another largely sleepless one) Frank woke up with an image in his head from the other side of wakefulness. It was a picture of a rotating lottery machine with a set of numbered balls which are delivered one by one to deliver a lottery winner. In his dream a ball had just emerged from the machine with 'Try' written on it. The balls were a strange mixture of molecules, ideas, people, all jumbled up and rotating.

A dream giving an answer. Ridiculous! But Frank stayed with it. He remembered the creative thinking course tutor saying something about being open to anything, the world out there, nature, dreams, books falling off shelves, anything. He was desperate, and the lottery machine image was an encouragement from his subconscious, he felt, to go back and let all the ideas, hypotheses and insights be jumbled up again. He felt the desire to throw it all up in the air and see what came down.

The real issue though at this stage was one of motivation. It was so difficult to build things up again. Real, deep down disappointment is so hard to transcend.

However, despite such reluctance, the lottery machine image got Frank's brain working again. He started to let the balls represent the molecules in a typical wash process. Could we do something creative with bleaches, enzymes and builders? Could we jumble the ingredients in a new way?

Or what about communicating what is going on at a submolecular level to consumers? He had looked through a spectrometer to see amazing pictures of how incredibly clever chemistry could remove dirt without damaging the fabric! These pictures could perhaps be used in a whole new approach to advertising fabric wash products.

The lottery ball led him to think too of a plastic container to hold the washing powder. It could deliver the powder steadily throughout the wash and accomplish what he had hoped for from the slow-release pill. It could also act as a convenient scoop, taking the powder out of the box, with some indication that the right amount was being applied. This latter point was particularly important as the company was moving to more concentrated powders. As a consequence, consumers were becoming suspicious; they felt they were not getting good value as in the past and were overdosing.

The wash ball gradually seemed to Frank and his team as having a lot more strength than was first apparent. They realized that if they went for it they might get two years in the market before the competition could copy. And the packaging team said it would be relatively easy to do.

At around the same time Frank had started to work in some real depth with consumers. They were helping him develop and refine a number of hypotheses. This work, along with an insight from other sources, had revealed a very interesting habit about the population of washers. Roughly half stuffed all the wash load into the machine without regard for whether they were white clothes, coloured, delicates or woollens. The other half made neat piles and had various segregated wash routines.

So the world was made up of either 'stuffers' or 'pilers'! What Frank realized is that the 'pilers' could get much better results if they used the various powders and liquids more wisely. The whole mentality of the business for 50 years had been to supply one product for all washes. But a 'piler' could get a much better wash if one product was used for whites, another for coloureds and so on.

STAGE SEVEN: THE REWARD

You know the 'Reward' is not because you have any proof or fact but because you get little confirmation from many different sources. All the bits seem to fit together and reassure each other. You know intuitively, your gut-feel informs but most of all it is a coming together. That 'Archimedes' effect, that Aha, is because the road is long travelled, it didn't just start in the bath.

– *The Hero has to resort to the metaphoric world to describe this stage. It is like seizing the fire (Prometheus) of the Gods, seizing the sword (Arthur) or finding the Grail (Celtic myth).*

– *All Hero can do is wait for it, ask for help, prepare mentally, establish a ritual or evoke a symbol or read great poetry. If it's right, it will happen. For the Heroic this is about waiting, passivity not action.*

Frank and the team liked this whole approach and realized that to deliver on this would mean engaging in 'dialogue' with the consumer to match actual habits with appropriate solutions. They thus developed dialogue tools, simple diagnostics, along with prototype 3-minute advertisement scripts to be shown late at night, infomercials, help lines, in-store expert systems. What this amounted to was a whole revolution in thinking (multi-products with explanation of category), a whole new way of talking to consumers (dialogue rather than monologue), use of new tools and new media (help lines, Internet, expert systems) and a new approach to advertising (no more patronising 'whiter, whiter, whiter', but a lot more information). It all amounted to a revolution in attitude and how the company did business.

Frank and the team really felt they had 'discovered' an innovative strategy that would reverse the slide in market share. Gradually they felt confident that they had found a way of delivering on many of the things consumers said they wanted. They were excited about it. It was new, it responded to the needs of the market place.

RETURN JOURNEY

Once a discovery has been made a very different set of problems must be faced. Foremost of these is that the 'discovery' is invariably a long journey of letting go of existing mindsets and attitudes, a sort of peeling off layers like with an onion. This 'letting go' is then complemented by the 'putting on' of new ideas, creating new hypotheses. The early hypotheses are invariably wrong so they go through a number of generations. When the final 'discovery' starts to come together it is as a result of many pieces falling into place like a 'shattered jewel' whose parts coalesce to form a remarkable whole.

It is not easy to tell of a journey of discovery in a board room. The only way Frank knew of communicating a journey was to resort to storytelling. Now the patience of most board members does not allow for much storytelling. What the board wants is proof. But how do you prove something that doesn't exist? Conventional market research has a very poor record regarding the truly new. Frank was well aware of failures that researched well: Ford Edsel 1959, Du Pont's Corfam, New Coke, RCA's video disk player. And all the successes that researched badly: the Xerox photocopier, 3M's post-it notes, the Sony Walkman.

STAGE EIGHT: REFUSAL OF THE RETURN

The whole process of the Journey of new encounter and discovery can be so engaging for Hero that the thought of Return to Homeground is simply awful. Hence, the Refusal of the Return. Hero just doesn't want to go back. Perhaps it is an unconscious awareness of the challenge now to be faced. Indeed the Return is typically as tough if not more so than the Withdrawal (Stages One to Seven).

- *Take action to keep alive the delicate, newly discovered, the Reward. The world way across the threshold is a strange world of surprises, ambiguity, paradox, emotional upheaval. The Reward will need protection. It is like anything newly born.*
- *Establish, ritualize a reconnection with the people and places that were encountered on the Withdrawal. The communication with others can act quickly to reconnect, inspire again, retract your steps to the Reward.*
- *Buy a copy of Homer's* Odyssey, *for it, above all, is the Bible for Returning Heroes.*

Conventional market research was not merely a poor tool, it could quite easily be totally misleading! Frank knew from experience that it generated vast amounts of data, most of which was useless, but some enormously helpful. It was the genius of the entrepreneur to know the difference. He was reminded again of the quote from one Albert Szent-Györgi. Indeed, he had seen what every competitor had seen. They all did the same market research. The art of innovation was in the creative interpretation.

But all this was his own internal rationalizing. He and his team knew the language of the board room. He knew the caution of the board members. Would they compromise? Would they be willing to spend a day with the same type of consumers selected at random? Would they make a similar journey to the one he and his team had made?

He tried this route. Surprisingly two or three of them were quite enthusiastic. Yes, they would be willing to meet consumers and even for a day. The rest responded by saying, in effect, 'I don't spend a fortune on the Market Research Department and outside researchers to have to waste my time actually talking to them. And anyway, I know what the consumer thinks; haven't I listened to over 100 research de-briefs?' They were impatient for a result. The second quarter results were disappointing. Innovation was one of the levers they could press to change things following two years of rationalizing.

In short, the board members did not sit down with consumers. Frank and his team were asked to present at the next board meeting. The board wanted the top 10 concepts tested and the results from the qualitative concept test.

What happened?

Well, Frank's designer came up with some superb design work on the 'ball'. The factory did a feasibility study. The technical team did some great work creating diagnostics for consumer dialogue. The advertising agency helped create visuals incorporating the 3-minute commercial.

They presented at 11.00 a.m. on 26 April. The board members were preoccupied by other matters. Two of them were only half listening to Frank and the team. The meeting finished before any decision was made.

There had been a half-suppressed laugh when Frank presented his lead idea of the wash ball. He did say too that the research results were somewhat inconclusive – some consumers loved it, others did not.

The response was basically hostile: 'You can't change consumer habits like that'; 'What will machine manufacturers say if we circumvent their delivery technology? We're trying to develop an alliance with them'; 'Won't it make a terrible noise as it bounces round in the drum? '; "US headquarters won"t understand because US washing machines load from the top, not the side'.

The response to the diagnostic was different. A few of them wanted it at once, but as a promotional device. They dropped everything else in the integrated strategy and wanted just one bit of it now. The only comment one made was that these new media were as yet unproven.

Frank experienced bitter disappointment. The gap between the year's work he and his network had done and the two hours the board gave him that day struck him acutely. Nothing was actually stopped. No decision on the concepts was actually made. But Frank sensed the board were not very happy. They saw no big 'breakthrough idea' in there. He had done damage to his credibility. It was as if they, collectively, had somehow decided he wasn't who they once thought he was. Nothing said explicitly or formally. It was just understood. The board closed ranks.

STAGE NINE: RETURN JOURNEY AND THE 'DEAD HERO' SYNDROME

You will be killed (not literally) on the Return Journey. Nothing that was genuinely new ever had an easy return. All you can do is to be prepared and to ensure that you are killed in such a way that resurrection is possible. The world will resist your 'gift', your 'grail', your 'fire'.

- *The very qualities that served Hero well on the withdrawal, such as openness, breaking boundaries, enthusiasm, naiveté and passion, are more likely to be liabilities on the way back. Be prepared to turn yourself round and become more political.*
- *Part of what Hero must prepare for is resentment, even envy that they were able to withdraw from the challenge of the day to day battle. To the warrior in the front line this will seem like a 'holiday'. The wise Hero waits out the challenges that essentially have nothing to do with their journey.*
- *Prepare a Return Journey action plan, working out who you will return with, when and how. Your role model is more Machiavelli and Odysseus than Achilles.*

Six weeks later, Frank decided to resign. He felt he had no future in the company. His rehabilitation would take too long. But more than the career, it was a matter of his losing faith in their ability to actually create something new.

POSTSCRIPT

Three years later things were very different. Word on the grapevine was that the wash ball was actually to be launched by a competitor. Suddenly the idea had real internal authority. All Frank's work was resurrected. The competitor did get to market six months earlier, so Frank's company had lost confidence to lead. In the meantime they had decided to redouble efforts on what they had always done – put a new stain removing chemical in. The consumer by now had become extremely sceptical, having been bombarded by advertising claims for years. This time the company put in two new chemicals for the 'best ever' wash powder. It actually was better at removing beetroot and Ribena (blackcurrant) stains first time.

The new formulation was launched with massive hype and hoopla. National campaign, regional campaign. Best ever. Whiter. Cleaner. Better.

From the consumer, there was a loud – so what!

From the trade, there was a loud – so what!

A set of discussions went on behind closed doors. The campaign was toned down. The new formulation was modified. It was now very similar to what went before. Circulating in the corporate underground was a message: the mountains heaved and the mountains roared and they gave birth – to a dead mouse!

It was cruel. But not without a grain of truth.

STAGE TEN: RESURRECTION, DEATH AND REBIRTH

There are various types of Return Journey. Every Hero will feel the pain of rejection (death). Some will respond by saying 'well, you don't like what I have to offer so tell me what you want and I will do it'. They let go of what they have learned. This is selling out. Another Hero decides they have had enough and leaves. They stay on the journey, stay with the world of new experience and drop out of job, cause or company. A third Return is to struggle to find a way back.

– *One great challenge for Hero is not to take the rejection personally. This is only exceeded by the challenge of putting up with the rejectors later taking credit once the idea is seen to work. The biggest test for hero is letting go emotionally of that with which they are passionately involved.*
– *Hold a little private* Wake *(an Irish funeral) for your idea. This Irish funeral ritual,* the Wake, *holds within it the two meanings of the word 'wake', death and waking up.*
– *Remember the old aphorism: 'You can achieve anything so long as you don't care who gets the credit.'*

A new chief executive came in. He started asking questions. Frank Price by then had been resurrected. Some people had never forgotten him. But the mainstream had started seriously to re-assess him. The re-framing of Frank was now a topic of conversation.

STAGE 11: RETURN WITH ELIXIR

As Hero lets go of their passionate, personal involvement with that which they have discovered, 'the Reward', they find others start to take it on and own it as if it were theirs. This is inevitable and appropriate. Others will likely be better at the refinement and implementation that is necessary.

- *Don't expect any public acclaim. The organization will probably have forgotten what you went through. And anyway, as a Hero, you are probably ambivalent about being in the spotlight. It will be embarrassing. Look for any recognition that you need from fellow heroes or your self.*
- *Read some Buddhist texts about the virtues of non-attachment, patience and letting go.*

But in terms of the company his energy, his contribution was now long gone. Frank was a 'dead hero'!

JANE LIPMAN'S JOURNEY INTO CULTURE CHANGE

Jane Lipman worked for Fifth Wave, a progressive computer technology company in a suburb north of Chicago called Highland Park. Fifth Wave had been in business for almost 20 years and employed nearly 300 people. It had always made money, though not much in the early days. Jane, a young married woman with two children, was in an administrative post and had been with the company for 10 years. She was not particularly confident but felt she had always done a good job for the company. In turn the company felt she was a very valuable, solid member, a good worker with a strong, attractive personality who added to the atmosphere in many ways. She was one of the people who might be described as the 'heart and soul of the company'. Many around her felt she had much more potential than she herself knew.

It was people like Jane Lipman that Dave Malley, the Chief Executive, felt would be real beneficiaries of culture change.

He had attended a conference on culture change in Chicago and had heard about empowerment, flat organizations, cross-functional, self-directed teams, teamwork, the untapping of creative potential. His judgement was that if these programmes could release the potential of some of the 'ordinary' people in his company, they would be world beaters. By 'ordinary' he meant people like Jane, who weren't whiz kid MBAs from Stanford or Harvard but who had real ability and, even though they were partly driven by divided loyalties to family and friends, were still capable of a whole lot more. He wanted extraordinary results from ordinary people. He wanted a way that they could 'surprise' themselves about what they could achieve.

Dave selected a consultancy to guide them through the process of culture change. In other words, the process would be focused on action projects and action learning. The idea was that various groups within the company would involve themselves in action projects which would enhance the company in some way. Such projects would include, for example, company induction, the company's logistics system, social activities, the raising of morale, how to make the company better known. Initially such a programme involves a briefing, explaining the process of the culture change movement. After the briefing, members of staff, hopefully, put their names forward as culture volunteers. Their training is geared towards their specific tasks, enabling them to become facilitators within their particular groups. A launch event brings together all these groups, elements of the various projects are discussed, and each group goes out to solve a particular problem, or come up with a particular solution, within a certain period of time. In this process culture volunteers learn much about themselves, about their strengths within a group, about their capacity to make a real creative contribution to the company.

This is the story of Jane Lipman's journey into culture change at Fifth Wave. It tells what went on in her head at different stages. It might be called the 'Inner World of the Culture Leader'.

INITIAL BRIEFING

The consultants commissioned by Dave Malley explained what was involved in the process of culture change. They outlined possible tasks, the process and the need for strong commitment from staff.

After the Briefing

Well, the consultants told us about it. Dave told us about it. They are all very enthusiastic, but it's very abstract indeed. All I get is, 'Other industries are doing it. We're in trouble if we don't do it.' But nobody seems to know what 'it' actually is. Only thing it reminded me of was a religious revival event. Talk of events, training and projects – we are asked to volunteer to work on projects. But what is this culture stuff? Fred, the guy in logistics, asked the consultant what culture was, and what our culture was. More babble. We were quite confused.

Later Reflection

I'm going to sign up. I am just so sick of sitting in the canteen hearing them moaning and groaning about the company. Knocking everyone. Knocking everything.

I'm going to sign up – never mind the cynics and the begrudgers. I believe Dave. I really think he is for the company and that this will help. He said it's a great opportunity for those who join in.

Well, I'll wait and see. But at least I'll have tried. I like Fifth Wave. It's been good to me. I'll do my best anyway.

The issues selected as tasks for the culture teams to work on were internally and externally oriented and included the following: internal communications, customer handling, an information booklet on all products and services, liaison with local colleges and the centralizing of logistics. Action on these projects would be expected within 180 days.

Even though the consultants did a good job there was still a high level of scepticism about the initiative. Quite a few members of staff had been burned by a quality circle initiative held five years previously. They were very cynical. They said that they didn't doubt Dave Malley's commitment but felt that middle management were not on board. The real issue was that no one was willing to voice these doubts too openly. When culture change was mentioned and Dave was in the room they would all say 'Yes'. Privately, it was a very different story. Jane was on the receiving end of some of this cynicism.

Early Days

> *I told 'em I'd signed up as a culture leader. You wouldn't believe the hassle they gave me. Bastards. It's as if I'm a Judas character – selling my soul to the Devil. They had a laugh at my expense, last lunch time, the canteen cynics.*

> *Oh God, will I actually be able to do it, head up a project, attend meetings? Hell, I hardly ever go to a meeting. It's all one-to-one for me. And they said I'll be leading a team, and the bosses are attending. Oh God, is there any way out of this? Wish I'd never heard of this culture rubbish! Why the hell did I put my name forward? Never again.*

CULTURE LEADER TRAINING

A two-day training session was held for those who had volunteered as culture leaders. It was designed to develop facilitating skills in people who might never have experienced group involvement. Jane was there.

The Training

> *Oh no! They actually want me to stand up and be a group facilitator. They call it process leading. This is even worse than I thought. I don't get it – bosses lead meetings, don't they, and what's this headlining, non-evaluation, in-out listening, excursions, group selection, climate setters? This is just getting worse and worse! Let me out. It's a nightmare. I'm trapped.*

Later Reflections

> *Holy cow. I survived. I actually made it. I actually did this Process Leading thing, on video; the group gave me 30 ideas and we seemed to get to a solution. The course leader was very positive (and he seemed genuine). There were a few things I messed up, but so what.*
>
> *Great. I can do it. But will I be able to do it for real at the conference?*

THE LAUNCH CONFERENCE

Jane's training was to help her act as a facilitator (or process leader as the consultant called it) at the launch conference at a resort hotel up near the Redwood forests. Her project was to do with the induction of new employees.

Most of the staff turned up and, after some presentations by Dave and the consultants, idea and concept sessions were held in groups of 15–20 people on particular topics. Each group was expected to present a result following two 2½ hour sessions. Jane was very apprehensive beforehand, but succeeded admirably with her group.

The Conference

> *We did it! We actually did it! The group were just great, incredible. A hundred ideas. Couldn't stop them. I was so scared, so nervous but my co-leader Ted was very helpful. 100 ideas, hard to believe. We helped our group do some lateral thinking, using the technique of mental excursion into other worlds (underwater and film) and that worked well. They selected priorities and we worked up a great action plan.*
>
> *We did it! I did it! I stood up in front of 15 people and delivered the goods. Never thought I'd 'see the day.*
>
> *Well the kids will bring me back to earth, but not just yet. What a star! I feel so good!*

THE FIRST TEAM MEETING

Back at base after the launch, Jane went about setting up the first meeting of her group. They had lots of work ahead. Their project, improving the induction methods of new employees, was quite formidable. The company had never actually formalized procedures. New staff were expected to find their own way around. It was tough on them. A definite process needed to be formalized which would dramatically improve the induction process. Jane went to her task with gusto, but found her team-mates less than enthusiastic!

Those guys, where are they? Phoned Pedro, the field engineer five times, three E-mail:s, and he hasn't responded. I'll kill him. At the conference he was great – tons of ideas, enthusiasm and now, no bloody reply. God damn it.

And the others, Sharon, Patrice, John, Ralph, no reply. Oh to be Dave Malley. One call and they all come running. Oh to be top honcho. I wonder is it me? Are they not coming to these meetings because I'm only an administrator? Damn them. But what can I do? They don't report to me. After all, Patrice is way up the organization. So what do I do? Cancel? Run it with 4 out of 15 members? What are they all doing? Are they really so busy? Why, oh why? And I still have those two reports to get in. My boss gives me heartache; seems to actually blame my involvement in culture change.

I've worked late three nights this week because of this culture thing. My kids are demanding and I even ended up last night having a flaming row with Stu. I'm so stressed out. Fighting fires on every front.

Why bother?

Two Months Later, Morning

Well, here at last. We sifted through our hundreds of ideas. We ran a little survey. Marvin (Mr Human Resources Director) gave us a hard time over this, said we were duplicating the consultants' survey and were asking loaded questions. He said that in the way we asked the questions we were implying the company was terrible at induction. Anyhow, reluctantly he let us go ahead.

Now is the day we'll test our proposal. Run it by Marvin. Give it a dry run. Hope we do better this time.

Didn't sleep too good last night. Woke at 4.00, dead worried. Just turned over and over. Was our idea okay? Surely it'll be okay?

PRESENTING THE PROJECT

Jane's team had considered many possibilities for improving the induction process: a mentor system, an apprenticeship scheme, a meet everyone evening, joiner's rituals. They finally decided on an induction leaflet, 'All you need to know about Fifth Wave'. It wasn't wildly exciting but at least they could produce it in the time allowed (they were expected to deliver in 180 days). They duly presented their proposal to Marvin, Human Resources Director, and came away feeling very deflated.

Same Day, Afternoon

The bastard. He shot me down. Total waste of time. Total God damn waste of time. This culture rubbish, total rubbish! They ask for our ideas. We produce, then they shoot us down! Marvin said he preferred the mentor scheme, thought the leaflet was a waste of time and money.

Those heavy cynics in the canteen were right, said it all along, it was a charade. Their advice was keep the head down. They told me it would all go away like every other initiative, quietly buried when its obvious failure becomes evident. *Oh hell!*

Same Day, Evening (at home with Stu)

Marvin! Why? Why did he kill it? Why did he pull me apart? Why did I have to hide in the toilet crying for half an hour? The bastard.

What is he at? Seemed to hint it was too expensive for the number of people involved. Hardly. Is he wanting to keep some of the employment benefits hidden from temporary staff? I just don't get it. He said he wanted us to do the mentoring thing. Said it was easier. But we had rejected that. We didn't think it would stick.

Anyway, I'm done with this culture change nonsense. Two months of hard work and hassle for this! And I think the others are fed up too. I spoke to a few other culture leaders. They were sympathetic but worried that the same might happen to them and some of them have taken on some really sensitive stuff like maternity leave and company environment/ health policy.

A SECOND WORKSHOP

An essential ingredient in the culture change process is continuous assistance for those involved. Jane found this second workshop particularly helpful.

After the Workshop

Didn't want any more training. I was so angry. Word had gone around so I wasn't alone. But then I got it. The consultant stuck up a chart about the 'Dark Night of Culture Change' and how tough it is. Yes, I was in that 'Dark Night', and I found out that a number of the others were too. I started to think, well at least I had got a response. Others seemed to be falling apart through apathy, or busy-ness.

The consultant got us to focus on what he called 'Docking Back'. Don't expect your project outputs to be accepted just because they are labelled as culture change, he said. They have to stand on their own merits. Top and middle management are in favour of change but so often seem to forget the connection between the initiative they've launched, the empowerment process they've started and the fact that this means junior people actually generating and developing ideas. Some management will reject your ideas. They will shoot you down. They forget that you have invested yourselves in the project.

You've got to be smart, he said. It's not smart to point out to top guys that there's a gap between what they say and what they do. After all they judge themselves on their intention, on their speeches, not on the effect of their behaviour on you. And by the way most of them suffer from the 'big ego' syndrome. They don't like being criticized.

The workshop was really helpful. I learned a whole set of new skills, consultative selling he called it. But I was still a bit angry. After all, the way the culture thing was set up it seemed like we were to be taken seriously, that we had a real possibility of changing things. And it was so embarrassing for me to be turned on like that by Marvin. It felt humiliating and I'm sure I've done myself no good in the department.

THE NEXT TEAM MEETING

Jane felt very buoyed-up by the training session. She had learned the skill of compromise and negotiation. The group decided to take what was worthwhile from Marvin's favourite option, the mentor idea, and modify it, incorporating much of their thinking of the previous few months.

After the Meeting

 Well, I got them back on track after the training. We had to let off steam for awhile. I lost two of my team though.

We're much smarter now. We'll go back to Marvin with a modified mentor concept as our proposal. We've learned to lose a few battles in order to win the overall war. Well, it wasn't really as if we were at war with the HR Director, but we did want to

get our ideas implemented. It had become a matter of pride and principle for us. Anyway, at this point we fed in our ideas behind the mentor concept. It was called 'A Guide for Mentor and New Recruit'.

CHECK-IN TO CULTURE CHANGE

The next big occasion was the Check-in. The consultants described the approach as Event Pull rather than Management Push. By this they meant that because no one wanted to look bad at a major company event people pulled out all the stops to make sure the projects happened. It seemed a clever way to get results. All the staff were invited, along with their families, to look at outputs from the projects. It looked like a market stall set-up, but it had the atmosphere of a county fair.

At the Check-in

Didn't think this would work and on a Saturday! I'm really surprised so many turned up. I like the teams' displays, the stalls. They're mostly very good. I'm impressed.

And ours? Well, not too bad either.

Highlight was when two engineers interrupted proceedings to do a Rap tune they had written with their own lyrics about the company, having a laugh at the journey we'd been through. It was brilliant.

Also, big highlight: bumped into Marvin at the barbecue. He half apologized. Said I'd got him on a bad day and the booklet idea was something that was duplicating work he had commissioned with some other consultancy. I said 'Why didn't you tell me?' He said, 'I didn't want to discourage you.' I said, 'Well you certainly did that!'

I had actually heard that Marvin had got stick from Dave Malley. Word had gone round about our meeting. Dave had told him off, said he was a blocker.

Three Months Later (at home with Stu)

> **"** *Well, was it worth it? Was the angst, the frustration, worth it? Was the hassle at home because I was so preoccupied and upset worth it?*

Yes, I'd do it again. I'd do it for me because of all that I learned through being involved, and the training. Very good. Even the 'Dark Night' idea was very good. The whole experience is a sort of initiation process as someone described it in the ideas session. I'm somehow initiated into a wisdom I could only have if I had travelled the journey. But it was really the near failure and the enormous disappointment when our idea was rejected that was vital. It was after that I sort of woke up. Before that, apart from the facilitation at the launch conference, which was scary, the whole process was like a cultural honeymoon.

But without the follow-up training I don't think I'd have pulled through. And I heard it was nearly cancelled! We had had a poor second quarter (was it because of culture change?), Dave was under severe pressure to cancel the whole thing, stop the training and get back to basics. Well, that training event was the turning point. I had totally given up on culture change. For me, it was dead. And I gather others felt just like me. It was always dead for a lot of people in middle management.

But Dave stuck to his guns, while under severe pressure. The training happened. We learned from crisis, pain, failure.

And yes. I'd also do it again for the people in the company. I really like them, well most of them. I actually feel different. I'm really proud of me, proud of the company.

And Jane was promoted three months later. She got a great job in customer distribution. She even agreed to give a presentation on culture change at the local Chamber of Commerce, which was very well received. Her confidence zoomed and so did her commitment to Fifth Wave.

STAGE TWELVE: HEROIC REFLECTION

The Heroic Journey may have transformed a company but most of all it will have transformed the Hero. The transformed Hero will have become a 'Master of Two Worlds', the world of the new, boundaryless, the experience but also the world of the established, bounded and the proven. From here Hero can delight in a choice:

- *Do it again (another Hero Journey)*
- *Guide others*
- *Become a King/Warrior*
- *Rest awhile.*
- *Read the last two pages of the book.*

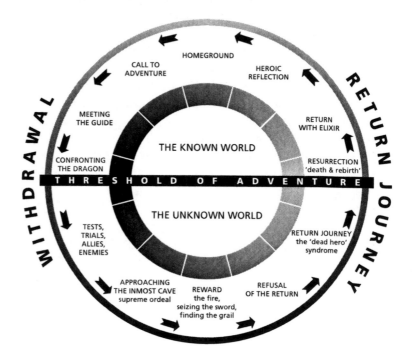

Fig. 3.1 The Heroic Journey: a journey of twelve stages.

4

THE RETURN JOURNEY

The Hero's Death (and Rebirth)

Redresser of wrongs, grasper
at golden shadows, Quixote
the knight is spurring his horse
– Michael O'Siadhail

THE RETURN AND THE DEAD HERO

The two narratives in Chapter 3 tell of the journey of two very different kinds of hero in the modern corporation. Frank Price is the bright fast-tracker who decided to take on the task of 'real' innovation in his company. Jane Lipman's priorities were as much in the home as in the business and yet she too decided to take on a task, albeit perhaps less ambitious, to change her company.

But narrative tales could have been told about any number of contemporary 'hero' figures: the new chief executive whose task is to fundamentally change a company strategy or culture, a young school leaver (or mature executive) who decides to set up on his or her own, a consultant in a service firm who puts in the 'unpaid' hours to create a genuinely new product or service.

Like Frank and Jane, such people will probably:

- be laughed at for trying
- feel personally stretched to breaking point
- struggle to keep up on other priorities
- have to sacrifice hobbies, social life
- suffer from symptoms of stress (sleepless nights, aches, palpitations)
- oscillate between elation and despair,
- and then, at the end, be misunderstood, ignored and have their 'discovery' rejected by those who rarely, if ever, take risks.

When an organization or a culture kills its hero(es) it usually hardly knows it has done so. Later reflection though will often reveal that someone really valuable and committed has resigned or that a key figure has become very cynical and is channelling his or her energies towards activities outside the organization. Hardest of all to accept is the fact that the hero was actually right. He or she saw something much earlier than the rest of the world did.

When an organization kills its hero(es) it does not impose a literal death, though to the hero it feels like that. Hero figures are sensitive – this quality tends to go along with the ability to break boundaries/mindsets, through creativity, intuition and an openness to the new. But heroes are also resilient. They will pick themselves up, knowing that disappointment goes with the territory. The intensity of the response comes in part from total personal and professional commitment to the task, to change.

When an organization or culture kills its hero(es), it also unwittingly strikes a death-blow to itself. It is the hero who brings back the stolen fire, the life-giving elixir which can save the organization. To destroy this gift is to sound the death-knell for the organization itself.

This is not a new story!

THE RETURN JOURNEY IN HOMER

The oldest epics we have left to us deal, in a major way, with the same issue. The epic oral poetry of Homer, contained in the *Iliad* and the *Odyssey*, are full of a rich array of 'dead hero' stories. Not many of the great warriors of the Trojan War have a successful homecoming; they call it *'nostoi'*.

Achilles' return

The Achilles model of heroism has been vastly influential in the Western world. Indeed, it still is. Here we have the great warrior, the great fighting man, and yet sown into the fabric of this greatness is a fatal flaw. It is the total single-mindedness that delivers super-human results, but also is the cause of the demise. This is the idea behind 'Achilles' heel'.

The *Iliad* is the story of Achilles' wrath, first over Agamemnon's insult and then over the death of his great friend Patroclus, who stands in for him in the fighting with the Trojans. Anger and finally revenge are driving forces behind Achilles' strength on the battlefield. Only at the end does he realize the tragic consequences of his single-minded anger. He meets Priam, the father of Hector, whom he has killed and whose corpse he has abused by dragging it around Troy.

Achilles never makes it back home. He knew this was the way things would evolve. He had a choice between a short but heroic life and a long but less dramatic one. He chose to live (and die) by the heroic code. This meant material rewards (the prizes of war) during life and in death the promise of immortality in an epic poem.

Hector's return

The chief fighter on the Trojan side also chose the heroic path. Hector defended his family (Andromache and their son) and the people of Troy. He was the embodiment of the heroic code, so clearly articulated by one of his soldiers, Sarpedon. This code meant fighting and risking death in the front line for which there was both fame and honour (*kleos*) and reward, especially material but also enhanced reputation (*timé*). After running scared from Achilles for a while, Hector returns to face his inevitable death.

As for Achilles, the reward was immortality, a life, short but heroic, deemed worthy of the Bard's song.

Agamemnon's return

The story of Agamemnon's return is revealing, but unsatisfactory. The king of the victorious Greeks does indeed return home. But what a return! His wife, Clytemnestra, murders him. She, no doubt, was furious that on his way to Troy, he sent for their daughter, Iphegenia, so that she would be sacrificed to the gods in order that the winds would blow. Perhaps the lesson here is to ensure that relationships are not soured by what the hero has to do to actually get to the reward. No hero can survive too many Clytemnestra figures on returning home.

The return of Menelaus

The Trojan war began when Paris effectively stole Helen, the wife of Menelaus, and took her and her wealth back to Troy. This violated the vital code, *Xenia*, by which guests were treated. In essence, Paris broke the rules of the game.

After the war, Helen was won back, the city of Troy was sacked but nothing was worked out between the two factions. No change, no movement.

The corporate world will often be attracted by the Menelaus' style return. It was essentially a return to the status quo, but somehow very unsatisfactory. Safe, but stuck.

Telemachus' initiation rites of passage

The myths, however, tell of some successful return journeys. Telemachus, the son of Odysseus, leaves Ithaca as a boy in search of his father and returns as a man. His is a classic rites of passage story. But, it is only through the divine intervention of the goddess Athena that he ever gets back. The suitors are quite intent on killing him. Without the gods being on his side, this would have been another dead hero story.

The successful return: Odysseus

Odysseus is one of the rare heroes who returns to the homeground. However, to do so he disguises himself as a beggar, lies repeatedly (to his wife Penelope and his father), engages in trickery (the Trojan horse) and has a ruthlessness that would make Machiavelli look tame. His killing of the suitors and execution of 12 of their ladies is one of the most chilling scenes in Western literature. And, by the way, on the way home every single one of his men is killed. Odysseus is hardly a team player. Here is a model of a cunning, wily, 'man of many ways'. No wonder feelings about Odysseus are deeply ambivalent.

The lesson from the Homeric corpus for the modern-day hero is clear. The great poet lays out a hero charter for such personalities.

HOMER'S HEROIC CHARTER FOR TWENTIETH-CENTURY BUSINESS

Requirements for avoiding the 'dead hero' syndrome:

- *Wisdom of Achilles*: the courage and fearlessness of a great warrior *but* without the fury and blindness that comes with obsession
- *Wisdom of Hector*: the ability to act bravely in situations of danger, doubt and ambiguity *but* the insight to know which battles to fight (i.e. do not fight Achilles).
- *Wisdom of Agamemnon*: the leadership skills to rally talent from many different quarters *but* to progress without sacrificing key relationships *en route* (i.e. do not sacrifice your daughter!).
- *Wisdom of Menelaus*: the humility to press on when shamed *but* not to ignore tough interpersonal conflict to ensure change is actually delivered (i.e. tough talking, two-way with Helen).
- *Wisdom of Telemachus*: the naivety to travel boldly into dangerous territory *but* the wisdom to know how vital is the support of the gods (i.e. Athene's hidden but essential protection).

- *Wisdom of Odysseus*: the openness to every experience under the sun and the political cunning of a great politician *but* does he really need to lie, beg and kill (i.e. make Machiavelli look tame)?
- *Wisdom of Penelope*: the patience and discrimination to wait under great pressure for the real thing (Odysseus not the suitors) *but* is there anything you can do to make your man less obnoxious!

THE RETURN IN THE TWENTIETH CENTURY: JAMES JOYCE

The Homeric corpus clearly lays out a demanding set of qualities for the modern-day successful hero. It is proposed to explore whether we have learned anything very much in the nearly 3000 years since Homer.

James Joyce, the great Irish literary genius, also worked with mythical themes in his epic journey *Ulysses,* which is the Latin name for Odysseus. Joyce explicitly picked this unusual hero and this story as the structuring device for his great modernist model. So, what insight can Joyce give us on the matter of the heroic journey and, in particular, can he help us to tackle the 'dead hero' problem?

History as circular

Joyce's *Ulysses* is less about withdrawal/return and more about spiralling round. For Joyce history was circular. Perhaps we need to see innovation in the same way. We will come back to old truths, to the same place, only deeper or higher than before. The journey is important, yes, but expect a lot of re-discovery.

Process innovation

Possibly the most remarkable thing about *Ulysses* is that Joyce uses a different style and technique for every one of the 17 chapters of a book that lasts the 24 hours of 16 June 1906. If applied to business, this system would give a company 17 different ways of looking at itself in 24 hours. Most managements are surely more like the one-eyed Cyclops in *Ulysses,* stuck with only one way of perceiving the world; appropriately so a lot of the time, but surely not when radical change is needed. *Ulysses* leads us, as do cubist painters, to look at the world from many angles.

Creative chaos

The Circe episode in *Ulysses* is a marvellous experience of chaos. Every way we have of making order in our world is systematically destroyed in Joyce's portrayal of Dublin's Night Town. The chaotic world of madness and laughter is nevertheless finely balanced and rigidly structured.

Mr Deasy's return

Mr Deasy is the bigoted headmaster in the Nestor chapter. Deasy is always harking back, always relating his current position to what happened before. Many of Joyce's most colourful characters were similarly stuck in a historical or mythical past: Evelyn in *Dubliners*, Joe in the Cyclops episode in *Ulysses*. Deasy's return is not a return journey in the Odyssean sense, more a return to a history/mythology that once was. How many headmaster/boss figures live in such a past? How many heroes fail to realize this reality, this enormous gulf between the time/era they are living in and the era of those in authority over them? Mr Deasy's past experience totally shaped his future. Return journey for him meant a return to the past.

Returning to Molly

The last chapter of *Ulysses* involves five very long sentences, unpunctuated, as we are taken into the head of Molly Bloom. Joyce gives us a full print-out of every single thought, past/present/future, sacred/profane, truth/fantasy, all muddled up into an ordered chaos. And during the journey inside Molly Bloom's head we find him wandering back to the 'golden age' of their relationship, way past the Blazes Boylan affair (and every other affair whether real or not).

There seems to be a message here for the contemporary hero to do like the great James Joyce and try to get inside the minds of those they seek to influence. Joyce attempted to re-create how a woman thought. The hero, to succeed on his or her return, must surely seek to enter the minds of those on the homeground.

Circe and the return

In *Ulysses*, both the father figure, Leopold Bloom, and the son figure, Stephen Daedalus, go into the chaos of Night Town in the Circe episode. Leopold sees himself being there as a guardian/protector rather than the willing participant that is Stephen. However, both are totally changed by the experience. There is no question of the father/boss figure sending off the son/hero figure while he stays home for the night.

Leopold Bloom did not merely stand by and observe his son's journey into the chaotic transformative world of Night Town Dublin. Observers are rarely, if ever, transformed. Active participants are. Innovation and change, Joyce is surely suggesting, is for participants.

The 'to not conclude' return

When you get right to the end of *Ulysses*, and indeed to every one of Joyce's short stories, you suddenly realize he has not concluded. All this great journey and no answer at the end. The author is almost stepping back and laughing: 'You, as reader, make up your own mind'. Scholars have argued for years as to the meaning of Molly's 'yes' at the end of *Ulysses*. Does she sleep with her husband again? Joyce does not spell it out. We have to form a point of view. We have to participate in the story. Joyce's genius, and challenge to us, is to enter in. To get anywhere with his art you have to travel with him. But at the end he gives no answer.

Perhaps Frank and Jane, in Chapter 3, failed to have the benefits of a Joycean, counter-intuitive, insight.

Never conclude on behalf of senior management. That is their job, but only after they have travelled along with you. And if you leave the ending open, they have to enter in, participate and, as a result, own the conclusions.

Conclude for a top management team and you will get a binary response, yes or no. Present with a more tentative tone and they have to become more involved.

Let us now create a Joycean manifesto on innovation and change using the literary device of inner monologue which Joyce uses in the last chapter of Ulysses.

JAMES JOYCE ON BUSINESS: THE INNOVATOR'S ODYSSEY OR THE WAKE OF INNOVATION

Innovation is as much about dying and death as it is about new birth my friend because unless there is a death of something many things even everything the journey does not ever begin and so we begin with a funerary ritual a wake celebrated in the grand Irish tradition at which we pay homage to a corporate corpse full of assumptions past successes arrogance serious hungry intensity facts proof technique methodology innovation itself truth track record. At this wake an odyssey can begin starting with the inspiration of a well told story many of them told by the mourners' jokes helped along by a deep reverence for the deceased and a generous helping of Jameson (the best) Guinness Baileys and the purity of Ballygowan's holy water for every story tells of experience past and to be and of what might be.

And well into the innovator's wake as the whiskey works its way the good mourners let go to a deeper reality and interconnectedness of all things life and death and meaning and nonsense and success and failure and somehow all the trivial and urgent of everyday working life are seen for what they are and in the grief there is a stirring deep down in the individual and collective belly as the seed of a thought a startling new way of living my our corporate life grows until I and we cannot avoid it no more and it carries with it no other authority than the authority of my gut my neglected intuition but I know it is right I just know and I think we just know. And my only problem now is to travel into the future past with those misfortunate enough to miss the innovator's wake because all present at the occasion were touched I know by the power of the community ritual wake and did wake to a deeper slower faster earthier like the corpses destruction way to live my our corporate life today everyday and by the inspiring grace of a story many stories told by the master bard(s) whose gift is that voyage into serious silly death birth innovate excavate extricate intricate defaecate regurgitate supplicate and find through an odyssey the gold at the end of the rainbow grail the holy one born life giving elixir fire of the gods paradigm blinding glimpse of a bloody good idea. And let go as the world wakes to a new possible blindingly obvious and not care who gets the credit takes it steals it jumps on it lectures about it and let go because another other is best fitted to take it on and mature the seed the life giving seed and only take credit from the humble band of loyal supporters bards of the corporate oral tradition who really knew who was there when the seed idea was reviled trodden on spat on laughed at and let go to the truth the new birth is about death and to remember the power joy sadness of the wake wake wake ...

DEATH AND REBIRTH OF HEROES PAST AND PRESENT

Frank Price's experience

When Frank Price reflected later on his experience he first of all pulled out a number of critical aspects of the journey. These are some of his reflections.

On head office

We did get away from national headquarters. You know what it is like, the vast open-plan office, 300 desks, 300 of the very best, so smart, so able, so professional. Enough electricity generated on that floor to light a small town. It ought to have been a great place for creativity, but it wasn't. They are all so polished, so professional, so aggressive. No place for a speculative thought, no place for a mistake.

On teamwork and himself

I think I was the worst teamplayer the company had ever seen, and the best, at the same time. I was so provocative and challenging. In company appraisals I was accused of being a bad team player. But there was a high level of trust within our team. We just seemed to know one another's thoughts. I think I played well within the team.

On guides and magicians

I think the word magician is grossly misunderstood. I see it as someone who can help you or a group move into very new places. My magician was Jack, an artist friend. I think what is vital with magicians is that they have themselves been into very new territory. Jack was also connected to all the great stories of history. He taught me to read myths and fairy tales allegorically, as a map. I think a magician/guide can help one stretch the mind, force one to open up and *seek out new experiences.*

On dragons and demons

We certainly fought the demons and dragons. Jack read a lot of the Swiss psychologist Carl Jung, so for him the dragon was all in one's own head. For me it was someone blocking my way in the company – Geoff Stiles for example. He kept blocking my way into research and all those scientists, though I got through that one eventually. I learned I had to come to an accommodation with the dragon. Behind the dragon's fire was hidden something precious.

On experience, not ideas

And we ended up in some very strange places. Jack kept pushing me to stretch. Stop going after ideas, he would say, what you need to have is new experiences. You have not lived through very much, he would tell me. You business people live in a very one-dimensional way. An idea without the experience has no roots. It will perish. Big ideas have deep roots; they are rooted in new experience. People at the top are very experienced too, but with very dated experiences.

On dark nights

Sometimes, often indeed, I felt it was all falling apart.

I just could not see where the project was going, where I was going. We seemed to be learning massively every day but the 'dark nights' as Jack would call them, the dark nights! We had very dark months on the project. Not many people can stand these dark nights so they don't take the risk of *going into places where they might happen.*

On shattered jewels

> **"** *But after the dark night it came together for us. We had a sort of project 'epiphany'. All the bits just seemed to fit together, like a jewel, a broken jewel coming together. Every fragment, experience, idea, mistake, somehow forming into a brilliant massive insight! We could see victory, money, wealth and fame ahead of us!* **"**

Frank also had some reflections on his involvement in the return journey.

Within Frank's power
Skillful will

There are three aspects of will and will-power, Frank learned somewhere – the strong will, the good will and the skilful will. It is not enough to have strong will and good will. Frank felt he had these in abundance. You have to have skill and cunning. The very virtues that enabled Frank (as hero) to get to the discovery – openness to what is possible, the capacity for breaking of boundaries, the willingness to live with fuzziness, chaos and ambiguity – these are all liabilities on the return journey. One core set of skills Frank felt he needed included consultative selling, multi-level, multi-function sales. One of his golfing friends was systems-selling in a large computer company and told him of a few courses.

The politics of return

Frank also felt he was really rather green on his return journey. A cynical friend sent him Machiavelli's book, *The Prince* and Anthony Jay's *Management and Machiavelli*. Yes, he could perhaps have benefited from adopting a less idealistic view of high-level corporate power politics. Perhaps it would have been a better working assumption to view the return as a game of power politics.

The liability of enthusiasm and passion

People in very senior positions, gathered in decision-making mode, are typically suspicious of enthusiasm. They are attracted to it but view it as dangerous. Enthusiasm is, however, ingrained in the character of a hero figure. Frank Price was a passionate and enthusiastic man. But this personal characteristic cost him dear in an environment that trusted fact and track record as credibility-winning criteria.

The unfortunate double bind in the territory of innovation is that by the time something is proven it has become old and probably well copied.

Not within Frank's power

Frank was quite philosophical about his experience. He had lost out back then. Time had proven him to be right. But it was too late.

He did feel senior management had to change as well. Most of all they had to come off the safe place of fact-based action, stop being detached observers and:

- travel some of the hero's journey;
- share the same new experiences;
- actually talk to consumers face to face, go shopping with them and regularly;
- go to events/rituals crafted by hero figures (not by the board-room);
- craft containable experiments in the market together with hero figures;
- listen to consumers/customers but do not impose responsi-bilities on them;
- act on gut feeling and intuition more than on fact.

Jane Lipman's return

In many ways Jane would not change anything with her jour-ney. It was tough, painful at times but, more than anything, a sort of waking up, as if shades fell from her eyes regarding herself and her potential, the company and its potential, and how complex systems work. She did have a few important re-flections on her return journey.

Avoid the authority of the change programme

By this she meant avoiding the assumption that because she was a chosen leader of the programme she could use this as a calling card on the return journey. Her position was essentially

'You must listen to me because I am a culture change leader'. She felt it would have been much stronger if she had let her proposal stand on its own well-thought-out merit.

Always leave bosses a way out

Jane realized that her tone had been one of 'take it or leave it' when presenting her group's conclusions. This left her boss in an embarrassing situation if he disagreed in any way with the proposal. He had felt there was no way he could get out of the situation without losing face. If he rejected the proposal, he would be painted by the organization as a blocker to change. If he said yes, he would be stuck with something that would cause him serious consequential problems. He was very unhappy with Jane (and remained so for a good while).

OVERALL REFLECTIONS ON THE RETURN JOURNEY

What this chapter has hopefully done is to highlight some of the great challenges there are for individuals or creative minorities who are serious about real change. The Homeric manual on corporate change presents a compelling statement of the difficulties. James Joyce, likewise, highlights the challenges but contains some hints as to possible ways forward. Reflecting on the contemporary narratives/myths of Frank Price and Jane Lipman likewise reveals what can be done.

The remainder of this book picks up the challenge in presenting various tools, innovation rituals and principles to help the hero and corporation succeed in their journey of change.

5

THE HERO'S TOOLBOX

Practical Ways to Survive the Journey

It is then the same story:
a bid to shortcut history
our scattergood craving for Eden?
– Michael O'Siadhail

CONTENTS

INTRODUCTION

If we attend to the great and recurring myths of the world, very often we hear or read stories of a journey. To apply myth to business is to suggest we can see innovation and change as a journey. However, unlike a modern-day business journey from, say, Frankfurt to New York or Jakarta to Sydney, the specific destination in an innovation journey is largely unclear, or at least couched in so many abstractions, e.g. innovate, grow, invest, breakthrough, that it is effectively unclear.

The hero's toolbox is required for just such a fuzzy, exploratory journey where I (broadly) know where I am, where I (broadly) know where I am going but where the destination will only become clear when I have travelled a good distance down the road. Much of the time the experience will be akin to the game where a blindfolded child has to find an object in a room. The directions of 'warmer' or 'colder' given by the other children indicate proximity to the object. All a hero can ever say is 'it feels warmer (or *colder*) ', as he or she travels into the unknown.

What are the kind of tools that help on such a journey?

Clearly no one tool will solve all problems. What works in one place will be useless in another. But tools there are, powerful tools, that can be learned, and can be used skilfully and strategically.

The proposed tools for the hero's toolbox are:

- *The Heroic Mindset*: this set of thinking tools provides core starting skills for any heroic quest.
- *The Hero's Road Maps*: maps outline the journey and can serve to forewarn or reorientate the hero when lost or confused.
- *The Hero's Process Toolkit*: modern-day business skills help the hero get the best out of a team when most of its members report to other people in the corporate monarchy.
- *Tools for the Return Journey*: this toolkit highlights the key players (in the homeground) who have to be won over if any journey is actually to be completed.
- *Symbols of Transformation*: powerful recurring images of transformation inspire and guide during the journey of innovation and change.

THE HEROIC MINDSET

In the heroic role of Frank Price in Chapter 3, Frank found himself reminded of the powerful learning experience during his study of Shakespeare at school. That learning process enabled him to develop an ability to be in an experience (in his case creating the ones about Shakespeare's *Hamlet*) and at the same time be a reflective observer of the experience. He was on an on-going, continuous learning journey.

Frank sought to apply this approach to every stage of his own journey into the world of innovation in fabric washing. Let us now attempt to make it explicit as part of our task of defining what we can term 'The Heroic Mindset' tool. What is the mindset appropriate to the hero's journey? Here is a starting hypothesis:

Create compelling hypotheses

Any innovation journey must begin with a large number of what might be called 'compelling hypotheses'. To be compelling the hypotheses have to be exciting to someone in the organization even if that person cannot fully explain why. Frank found himself far more interested in a person's passion and enthusiasm. Latterly he created a few posters for his office: 'Passion over fact'; 'Innovation – an ounce of enthusiasm over a ton of fact'; 'What are you excited about?'; 'The journey into what doesn't exist – yet'.

The training Frank received in creativity was also very helpful in creating 'compelling hypotheses'. The term hypotheses was chosen over the term ideas. It somehow gives so-called 'ideas' a higher status and gets round dismissive clichés like 'ideas are a dime a dozen'.

Run exploratory experiments

The hero's journey now moves on to the stage of 'exploratory experiment'. The term 'experiment' was helpful because it conjured up the tentative, learning focus of the journey. Putting the term 'exploratory' together with experiment was important because innovation experiments can never conform to the norms of a controlled scientific experiment such as in a laboratory. Innovation experiments cannot be fully shielded from the effects of confounding changes out in the environment/market.

The phase and mindset of 'exploratory experiment' is about playing with the hypotheses in a simulated situation in order to get a feel for a thing. It will not get proof. It will not get facts.

Frank had tried hard to convince his board of how notably unreliable conventional consumer tests were when applied to the genuinely new. He listed a number of well-known successes that had tested badly and a number of well-known failures that had tested well. It made no difference. His board was suffering from a bad case of 'enchantment of facts'.

His argument for intuitive decision-making based on a direct experience of the journey of competing and completing hypotheses and a series of well-crafted 'exploratory experiments' fell on deaf ears.

The heroic mindset is about a continuous journey of a number of single but powerful steps:

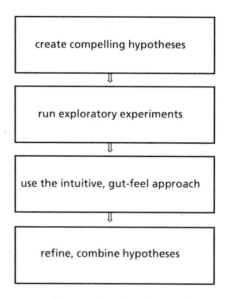

It is a process, not a destination. Its focus changes from withdrawal phase to the return journey phase.

The heroic mindset can be applied to technical challenges, people challenges and corporate challenges. It was a central orientation for Frank's journey into innovation.

For our other hero, Jane Lipman, the whole journey was just so new, it was more a case of being 'thrown in at the deep end'. She, however, implicitly adopted the heroic mindset in her hypothesis that things could be improved and in her willingness to participate in the exploratory experiment of the culture change project.

THE HERO'S ROAD MAPS

No map is a substitute for direct experience. No map can capture the richness, the perspective, the wholeness that comes with moving directly into unknown, uncharted territory. But a map has its uses. It acts as a simple outline against an experience that can be almost too rich, too full of detail. Most importantly, it lays out the pathways, the options and the possible ways back to base when the explorer hero is caught in a maze of uncertainty. It is never the territory itself.

Two maps are relevant to the hero's journey. The first of these (Fig. 5.1) captures the simple yet powerful essence of the journey. It is useful primarily as a tool for dialogue. It provides a basis for communication and understanding between hero and organization. It enables the innovator, the hero, to communicate to the organization his/her need to move away from mainstream operations, from day-to-day pressures, in order to think and explore new ways. It also enables the hero to indicate something of the necessary vagueness associated with exploration and discovery.

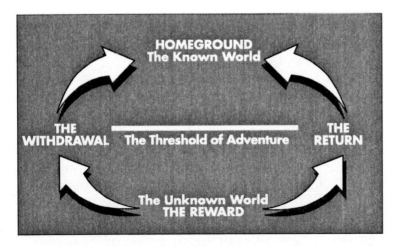

Fig. 5.1 The journey: withdrawal and return.

This map allows for mutual give-and-take in terms of internal communication. Those staying in the homeground can express their point of view. To them the journey can appear almost irresponsible, an indulgence. They observe the innovator/hero and the enjoyable, exciting aspects of the exploration, and may resent the fact that they must keep the home fires burning, working relentlessly to keep the business going on a day-to-day basis. The map perhaps helps in making what is happening, explicit.

The tool of dialogue is most crucial for the return to homeground. The myths of history tell of far more 'dead heroes' than of successful returns. Those who make it home are either very lucky (Telemachus) or very ruthless, using disguise and lies to protect themselves (Odysseus). The return, as both Frank Price and Jane Lipman discovered, is a tough and perilous process. Innovator and organization must consider how exactly they will reconnect. The dialogue process here could perhaps appropriately result in a contract or charter covering the appropriate rewards and protections to be offered to those who undertake such a journey.

The second map (Fig. 5.2) is more for the use of innovator and team. It outlines the various stages of a typical journey.

The first stage is *preparation*. Here the hero explores the implications of leaving the homeground, examines the 'yes' voices and the 'no voices'. This is normally a time of upheaval and vacillation. The temptation may be to hold with the status quo, but alongside that is the lure of magic: Come with me, let's search for gold. The natural ambivalence of this time leaves the innovator in a state akin to that of Tolkein's hobbit, Bilbo Baggins! Bilbo has a nice comfortable life, his lovely house and gardens, all his friends around. Life is very cosy for him. Then suddenly Gandalf comes by to tell him he must go on a journey. The 'no' voices come loud and clear to the comfortable hobbit. Bilbo has experienced the 'call to adventure' and he is none too happy.

The call might be from an outside source, a friend, a chance encounter, a boss. Or it might be a nagging voice from within,

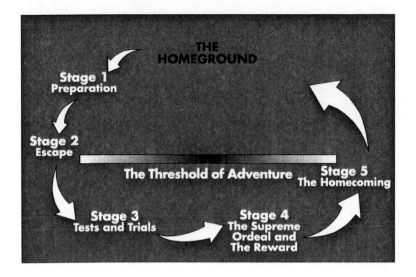

Fig. 5.2   The journey: key stages.

a voice that keeps urging, 'Things can be different. Things can be better'. Response to the call must initially involve ambivalence, the yes and the no, at the same time. The innovator's 'yes' must be strong and determined because sooner or later the chorus of the world will clamour, 'Why?' 'What for?' 'Aren't things OK as they are?' and so on and so on!

The preparation stage is typically about getting in the right state of mind, balancing the 'yes' and the 'no' but finally making the decision.

Once the decision has been taken to go on the unknown and uncharted road, the innovator must learn certain skills, depending on his/her particular circumstances. Frank Price attended a creative thinking event. For him the approach of developing hypotheses was a connecting thread which held him right through his experience. Preparation also means finding a guide and the right kind of helpers.

Stage 2 is the escape. The hero must get away from the mainstream, away from the pervasive culture, the existing attitudes and mindsets. It is a mental more than a physical escape. This is the stage of confrontation with the dragon, the guardian of the threshold. The dragon guards its territory fiercely and can be overcome only by the greatest of subtlety on the part of the hero. Frank Price found the dragon in the person of Geoff Stiles, Head of Technology and Development, a man determined to protect his area. The dragon can also appear in the guise of internal doubts and negative self-image; there it is personal, internal uncertainty which holds back the innovator. The voices echo the obligatory 'should' and 'ought', not the passionate 'want' and 'will' which is the stuff of utter determination.

This third stage in the journey, tests and trials, depicts the many and varied obstacles that face the hero. In the world of myth, the hero is invariably tested along the way. He must bear with the many trials, suffer unimaginable pain, heartache, disappointment. They might lose their way, might experience shipwreck, might lose all their companions to the sword or the wilderness. And still survive and push on to journey's end. The innovator sees these images as metaphors for what in the business world might be technical, marketing, personnel or financial problems, problems which must be overcome if the process of change is to be effective. Some of the tests and trials may be directly related to the fact that the innovator's task is often so little understood by the organization. Frequently and unknowingly it may put many additional tests and trials in the path of the searching innovator.

Stage 4 deals with the supreme ordeal and the reward. At a certain stage the hero feels as if the whole integrity of the journey is falling apart. This is a time of enormous frustration and fear, a 'dark night' of despair. It is, however, the prelude to insight, to the coming together of all the bits and pieces, the 'shattered jewel' reforming or perhaps forming for the first time.

Finally, Stage 5 relates to the homecoming. Will the hero be welcomed like the 'prodigal son' or experience yet further dangers? Agamemnon, it will be recalled, was killed at this stage, while Odysseus finally reached Penelope in spite of the very real threat of suitors. The innovator's grand plan can collapse at this point, as it did temporarily for Frank Price, if those on the homeground are not prepared to listen. The map serves as a forewarning.

THE HERO'S PROCESS TOOLKIT

Central to the notion of innovation and change as a journey is a set of skills that are more about 'how' to think (process) than 'what' to think (content). These skills were important to the hero figures in both our stories (Chapter 3). We have examined how Frank adapted the creative thinking skills to make explicit what we called The Heroic Mindset. We have also examined the process skills that were as vital to Jane Lipman on her journey. Jane had rarely attended corporate meetings, at least of groups of five to twenty people. Her briefings were largely on a one-to-one basis. She needed experience and skills on how to run a creative meeting of nearly 20 people to get her project started. She needed basic group facilitating skills.

The following is a composite set of skills for the Hero Toolkit, using modular training inputs run at appropriate stages in the journey.

Module I (2/3 day) (for the withdrawal phase)

- *Creative problem-solving:* how to run a group to generate and develop ideas.
- *Design making/conflict resolution:* how to structure a group to take high quality decisions and resolve conflicts.
- *Project planning:* a group-based approach to project planning to ensure all participants have ownership of the plan, having created it together.

The teaching method most appropriate to hero figures is 'learning by doing'. Jane had to stand up, lead her group (initially in a training setting) to generate and develop ideas on a real company task. No case study, this was a current issue in one of the departments. The approach was plan–do–reflect and the style therefore one of 'reflection in action'.

Module II (for the return journey)

The core toolkit for returning heroes is dealt with under 'Surviving the Return Journey' (see below). The skills needed can be entitled: 'Large Account Selling Skills'. These are the selling skills which are needed by people like computer systems sales people, consultants, etc., who have to sell to an organization rather than a person. These involve winning over a number of different types of people at different levels.

To do this within a monarchy is particularly challenging because outsiders can cross levels and functional boundaries very much more easily. However, the process is quite similar whether used by outsider or insider.

Essential reading for returning heroes is Homer's *Odyssey*, Machiavelli's *The Prince* and Sun Tsu's *The Art of War*. This will help the hero to understand the mentality of those very different characters (warriors, guardians, kings) who typically populate the homeground (see Appendix for further proposed reading). Indeed a composite toolkit of all the skills of Odysseus, Machiavelli and Sun Tsu would constitute excellent material for a hero/innovator's MBA.

TOOL FOR THE RETURN JOURNEY

Key players

Myth and personal experience highlight the real challenge facing the returning hero. It is so easy to end up as a 'dead hero'.

The essential survival tool for the hero is a set of descriptions of the very different mindsets of the key players to be met on the return journey. The key players who will play a role are recognizable in the world's myths.

We will briefly describe the key players and key helpers. The characteristics and guidelines for them are summarized in Figs 5.3 and 5.4. An extra section highlighting challenges for the hero is included in Fig. 5.3. Heroes need this help because they tend to find some of the key players particularly difficult.

One note of caution is appropriate here. Typecasting in this way can be somewhat simplistic; it holds the real danger of categorizing people into various boxes. And, of course, it must be remembered that different situations will bring out different characteristics in people. A person can be a hero at one point in time and a warrior at another. Nevertheless, it is possible to talk of particular types of people who become focal points in the process of change, and the language of myth offers a rich lexicon with which to do it.

The king

Ultimately the king determines what happens in his kingdom. How significant it is, then, that so many of the ancient myths portray a wounded king, presiding over what T. S. Elliot would describe as a 'wasteland', an impoverished kingdom. Moving on from mythology, we can speculate on how many contemporary 'kings' are wounded, and how many preside over a corporate 'wasteland', one that is not capable any more of change, of innovation, of anything generative. In Greek myth, this is Zeus, the all powerful, but in corporate life one whose power does not destroy the Promethean energy of the hero figures. Frank Price's organization had two styles of leadership. In the first failed return, after which Frank left the organization, the king, the then president, could be described as a king/warrior rather than a king/hero. His natural empathy was for the warrior types. He felt most comfortable with them. The new president was much more a king/hero leader. His empathy tended towards a character like Frank.

The type of king an organization needs will depend on the state of its development. The myths suggest that the king's primary responsibility is to ensure that the kingdom is fertile (surely a metaphor for profitable!). In earlier times the king was removed if he was no longer generative. 'The king must die', became a tradition and was usually acted upon as a recognized institution.

Today's king must mediate between the demands of the hero and the demands of the warrior. Without the balance, no kingdom, no civilization, no business will survive. In practice, this will often mean ensuring that the predominant warrior culture

	KING	WARRIOR	GUARDIAN	CRAFTSMAN
Mythical Character	Zeus	Achilles	Apollo	Hephaestos
Basic Mindset	● Focus on the 'Big Picture' ● Mediate between many conflicting demands especially hero and warrior ● In myth responsible for the kingdom's generativity and fertility	● Focus on tomorrow's battle and the war ● Goal, result and action orientated ● Comfortable with people, tools, procedures proven in battle ● In myth, needs to be aware of their tragic flaws	● Focus on protecting what exists today ● System and procedure and principle orientated ● Safeguarding what we have now and avoid mistakes ● In myth, associated with structures (temples) to get people thinking on higher things	● Focus on making things ● Pragmatic, feet on the ground but capable of practical creativity ● Efficiency, predictability, reliability keep him awake ● In myth can make objects of beauty and functionality ● If you take the Guardian on you will almost always lose

Challenge for a Hero	• Be aware of the difference between what the king says and what the king does • What the king says (e.g. about innovation) may not be what keeps the king awake at night (e.g. results)	• No warrior risks his people or the outcome of a battle on unproven weapons • But all warriors love to see more powerful weapons • Find a way to get warr or to experience the power of new	• This person does worship a very different god from you, not better or worse, just different • Swallow your pride and become a co-traveller with your opposite	• You are upsetting the Craftsman's plans, efficiencies, etc.; expect a response • The Hero in the Craftsman could very well be your saviour • Access their practical creativity
Key Guidelines for Hero	• If King/Warrior – probably keep King/Warrior out of picture until you have some positive results • If King/Hero – involve right from the start and keep briefed throughout the Hero Journey	• Keep your credibility with key warriors through withdrawal phase • Timing is everything. Get space in between battles never at heat of battle • There's a heroic core in every warrior, give it space to emerge	• On procedure (e.g. expenses, budgets) be squeaky clean • Use logic to argue for a non-logical approach • Actually seek out and 'embrace the dragon' • Meet privately first, not in a group	• Involve as early as you have a 'strong hypothesis' • Don't let existing investments totally dictate how things are made • If you really believe in your idea fight for the new (and defendable) way of making it

Fig. 5.3 Surviving the return journey: the key players.

which is essential in any mature business leaves some kind of space for minority 'hero' figures. The king must protect the hero and act in such a way as to ensure the success of the return journey.

The warrior

It is the warrior figure who invariably survives and thrives in the modern corporation. The hero will certainly encounter warriors. These are the people fighting today's battles, with today's tools. They are the people whose primary task is to ensure that there is a homeground there when the hero does return. In Greek myth this figure is best epitomized by Achilles, the archetypal warrior for nearly 3000 years.

Warrior characters are typically very action-oriented. They push for results. They are focused, aggressive, good team-players. They also tend to have a low tolerance for the ambiguity and disorder that is so much a part of the innovator's journey.

Warriors can sometimes feel contempt and suspicion for the hero. They can assume a 'Were you on holiday?' attitude. Credibility comes from the last battle fought (and won). For the warrior, it is the battle won which delivers credibility, and this means a voice that will be listened to. The 'test and trials' and the 'supreme ordeal' of the hero's journey is not a battle in warrior terms. And worse, the 'discovery' the hero delivers is likely to be seen as unproven, speculative and even half-baked.

Geoff Styles was one of the warriors in Frank Price's story. For much of the time Frank dismissed the warriors. He felt a contempt for the often bureaucratic, system-driven manner in which they operated. He was also critical of their political nature and their reluctance to challenge the existing system. Yet in time he came to appreciate their vital role.

Clearly, it is essential to be able not only to recognize the roles the 'hero' and the 'warrior' play on the innovation journey, but to mediate the negative way they will tend to view each other. Without this no innovation journey will succeed.

The guardian

The guardian is an essential player in top management in any organization and indeed throughout it. The focus for guardians is primarily to act as a 'safekeeper', to protect the corporate assets. They like to set up or have in place standards and procedures and then to have systems to ensure they are followed. The Greek god of the guardian is Apollo, the god of order and structure.

They will often be the sceptic sitting in the corner of the boardroom ensuring that hard facts are produced to support every decision. They can act as gatekeeper to keep out salesmen and consultants who they feel are intent on helping themselves to the corporate funds. But they also serve to maintain core assets: financial, procedural, product/brand, etc.

It is very easy for the hero to polarize with guardians and become their enemy. The hero's personal strengths are the guardian's weakness and vice versa. Heroes ignore boundaries, systems, procedures and are comfortable in a world of ambiguity, paradox and change. All this is anathema to the guardian.

However, smart guardians also know the commercial value of the successful intuitive leap. Providing them with a rationale to be irrational (or at least willing to proceed without proof) may mean turning an enemy into a valuable ally. The wise hero remembers the mythical counsel to 'embrace the dragon'.

The craftsman

These people make things. They will actually create the product, the packaging and the process to reproduce the same output over and over again. In Greek myth this is Hephaestus, the master craftsman who made the famous shield of Achilles, a creation of functional and aesthetic excellence.

Like the guardian, craftsmen are essentially pragmatic, with their feet on the ground. They are, however, more interested in making a product than the procedures needed to run a business.

The real art of the craftsman is to stretch the possible, to see just what can be done with existing assets and investments. He or she must also deal with the front-line production people for whom anything new is a direct challenge to the efficiency of the current manufacturing system and for whom innovation is a monumental nuisance. So the craftsman must be a pragmatist, a salesperson, a diplomat, an engineer of people and things, a politician and indeed a friend of the hero – clearly a very vital quasi-heroic role.

It is easy for the craftsman and the hero to polarize. They simply have different short-term priorities in most corporations. However, the wise craftsman will listen to the hero and seek to find a way to make what could well be the company's future, while at the same time safeguarding existing assets and investments. Past investments, especially in plant and machinery, can create a myopia. A great craftsman knows when to move on and not let existing factors threaten the future. A wise hero, on the other hand involves the craftsman early in the process.

Key helpers

In the myths of the world there are helpers of so many different types that appear and disappear having vitally helped the hero on to the next stage: the old and ugly crone, the frog that the princess must kiss (before it transforms into a prince), the small animal who is helped and yet later rescues the hero in the same way.

The general message seems to be to accept help from whatever source, whenever, wherever and to be open to it. Indeed, perhaps seek it out among the discarded, the rejected, the ugly, the unpopular. In a corporate setting there will be a great deal that would fit one or other of these categories, be they ideas, people, things.

There are, however, other more recurrent and central sources of help. These are:

- the guide/magician,
- the bard,

- the fool,
- the friend.

The guide/magician

What a guide does in the myths is help create an event at which transformation happens. One of the great guide/magicians is Merlin in the Arthurian legends. Merlin orchestrated the ritual of the sword in the stone at which the rightful king of England was elected. Merlin was a king-maker. Merlin was a creator of a transformative ritual.

In Jane Lipman's fifth wave the senior management and change consultants crafted the event at which the culture change was launched. They created a powerful 'seeding' ritual occasion for a journey of change to begin. They also created one four months later, which was equally important for Jane. Frank Price very much regretted the absence of transformative ritual occasions. The board meeting was, he felt, an ancient dated ritual which served to preserve the status quo. It was not an event, a ritual suitable to his task. It was, as he saw it, the moment of his demise. The board meeting created 'dead heroes'.

The task of the guide/magician is to craft transformative rituals. The real irony in their craft is that they create an ordered set of behaviours in order to encourage the group to move into new space, into places they have never been before. The guide/ magician ironically creates a highly structured process in order to free up the content, free up what people think and do.

The guide as such played a minor role in Frank's story. Frank was increasingly thinking that perhaps it was a vital ingredient that was missing in his company. Every ritual seemed to preserve the status quo and reinforce the existing hierarchy. They needed transformative rituals to free them. The guide/magician was a person with skill set to help orchestrate these. He was also developing a hypothesis that the really memorable parts of any journey are the events at which people gather and not the journey between point A and point B. This calls for an innovation journey which must be marked by truly memorable events/rituals. These events create the stories, and create space at which stories could be told to inspire the journey into the unknown.

Mythical character	MAGICIAN/GUIDE **Hermes**	BARD **Odysseus/Homer**	FOOL **Satyr**	FRIEND/COACH **Various (animals)**
Basic Mindset	● Focus on orchestrating occasions where resolution, surprise, break-through happens through their subtle interventions. This can feel like magic ● Comfortable with a humble, at times invisible role once events/meetings are running well ● In myth, the character who drifts in at critical moments to make something happen ● Guides innovators through dark nights of doubt, despair and confusion	● Focus on passing on wisdom or shaping current events through myth and story ● An ousider/insider who helps articulate what hasn't been said but is strongly felt by many ● Embodies the spirit and soul of an organization or culture ● In myth, the teller of the story, usually a known story shaped for current events	● Focus on acting out the madness, stupidity or a culture through exaggerated humour ● Dangerous dance, because their message is often very close to the bone ● Fool/Wisdom, close partners ● In myth, many forms but in Greek myth, explicit role in Comic Festival	● Focus on help for young hero and advice as to how to survive higher levels of organization ● Accepted at top levels and all levels often because no threat to powerful ● In myth, friends and helpers come in many strange guises

Key Guidelines for Hero				
	• Use guide/magician to help shape key events and occasions on the journey. In modern parlance also called Process Consultants • Guides can temporarily relax the hierarchy (e.g. round table events) or invert the hierarchy (world upside down). Very useful on return journey • Use to create temporary chaos and disorder to enhance creativity; network; shape your journey	• Tap the bard's fund of knowledge to find out about previous Hero Journeys and past dead heroes. Bard will tell by stories how things really happen • Bard can open doors or close doors so ensure you have them on your side for contacts • As hero, you are probably material for their future stories so give them the inside track	• Try to get senior executives to sit face to face with their consumer/customers to create the 'King meets Fool' effect • Christmas parties: perhaps dress up, use satire and humour to act out excesses of the organization • Cartoon in in-house magazine • Resurrect the fool as transformer	• Cultivate friends at all levels during withdrawal phase of the journey. They could be vital to your return journey • Friends will tell you what to say, how to say it and when to say it

Fig. 5.4 Surviving the return journey: the hero's helpers.

The bard

Before we learned to write, we told stories to each other. The great Homeric epics were passed on through a rich oral tradition by the bards. Now we have learned to write, and most corporations are becoming written cultures, yet we still tell stories. They are the means by which the informal, unwritten culture of a company is transmitted. Stories are how the unpopular, the unsayable, the mistakes, the madness and stupidity of corporate life are transmitted. Anyone seriously interested in innovation and change who ignores the oral culture does so at their peril. Any consultant report separated from the stories and the oral tradition will invariably be ignored as irrelevant.

It is the bards, the storytellers who keep alive the oral tradition in every company in the world. The bard may occasionally be in a position of formal power but more usually occupies a pivotal position at some nodal point in the company. They have the 'power of the powerless'. Their lack of formal power gives them access to all the stories, all the experiences and feeling around them. They, more than anyone, keep alive the culture of the company; they can determine which changes succeed and which fail because they shape the oral tradition, the informal culture.

Mario Lhosa's *The Storyteller* depicts the contribution of story and storyteller in a very powerful way. His book tells about the Machiguenga tribe on the Amazon in eastern Peru. This tribe lives in small, isolated units spread over a vast area of the jungle.

They never settled, never built a village, being on the move all the time. In their culture, a vital role is played by the *hablador* (the talker or speaker). According to Lhosa, the *habladores* provided:

> *something like a courier service to the community. Messengers who went from one settlement to another in the vast territory over which the Machiguenga were dispersed, relating to some what the others were doing, keeping them informed of the happenings, the fortunes and misfortunes of the brothers whom they saw very rarely or not at all. Their name defined them. They spoke. Their mouths were the*

connecting links of this society that the fight for survival had forced to split up and scatter to the four winds. Thanks to the habladores, *fathers had news of their sons, brothers of their sisters and thanks to them they were all kept informed of the deaths, births and other happenings in the tribe. [In short,] the simplest, the most time hallowed of all expedients, the telling of stories, were the living sap that circulated and made the Machiguenga into a society, a people of interconnected human beings.*

Ironically, as modern business becomes ever more global, full of flexible, ever-changing structures, temporary, ritual teams, perhaps it is starting to resemble increasingly the Machiguenga! But more immediately relevant is the role of the *hablador*, the bard. It is the bards who keep alive the culture. They are the living sap that hold the society together.

In the context of our innovation story, Frank Price had made extensive use of bards in his journeys around the company. He, however, lacked a political bard who could have helped shape his return journey. This bard could have coached him on how to return, when, with whom, in what sequence, etc. Jane had access to Fifth Wave bards who helped ensure her survival within the system.

The fool

In the medieval court there was always a place for the fool, the clown, the trickster. The fool somehow had the space to say what everyone else was thinking and feeling but no one was saying. Such a person could confront the king with the vital gap between what was said and what was then done.

In the Grail story, Parsipal is the naive one who alone can unlock the key to the Grail. This is a powerful idea. It has echoes in Christian myth where the stories advise 'becoming like little children'. In popular storytelling this is the *Emperor's New Clothes*, the story where only the child shouts out what everyone else can see but cannot say. Yes, 'the King is in the altogether! [the nude]'.

Frank saw the consumer as the fool. Their real value he felt was not that 'consumer was king' but that 'consumer was fool'.

Now clearly this was not in any sense that they were stupid. It was more in the sense that they didn't know corporate politics.

They were completely unaware of how important someone was in the company. Frank remained convinced that he was right to set up an event at which the bosses would meet the consumer. This we could now call a 'king meets fool ritual'.

What would happen is that the consumer would say what came naturally. Consumers were like Parsifal, naive. It was so different from the warriors who surround the king, second guessing what they think the king wants to hear.

Frank never succeeded in crafting this potentially transformative ritual. The kings (and warriors) refused to turn up. He failed to change how they thought and worked. They (the kings) remained with their old-style rituals, and as a result heard no new stories. They blocked out the possibility of creating a new myth for their company.

The friend/coach
This is in some ways so obvious it seems hardly worth saying. Except that hero figures are so often so caught up in their journey that they can be very sloppy about cultivating relationships. The myths frequently highlight how vital help can come from the strangest sources.

Friends/coaches can be central in guiding the hero on the return journey in terms of how to get their argument across, how to present their discovery in a way that people (kings, warriors, guardians) can actually hear it. Wise heroes move forward, building their network.

SYMBOLS OF TRANSFORMATION

In the world of myth certain symbols recur, symbols of transformation. Frank realized the importance of using these as reference points in the process of innovation. They would form part of the language that he and his colleagues needed to learn in order to work most effectively in the area of innovation. Symbols have power to communicate and move people in a way that words do not. Symbols also have the capacity to surmount cultural and language barriers, just as music can.

From the hundreds of symbols that litter the world of mythology, we have identified six that are particularly relevant in the context of innovation.

Enchantment or dream

Myths tend to portray the world and its inhabitants as being caught up in an enchanted or dream-like state. The task of the hero is to break the enchantment, and by so doing to allow the kingdom to live again and to move forward. Frank failed to break the various enchantments – the enchantments about what they thought, how they thought it, why they thought. He was treated as if he was living in a 'dream' and out of touch.

An organization can become enchanted by its previous successes. The complacency of success can cast a spell which prevents people from moving forward in radically new directions. They become prisoners of a certain way of thinking and doing things, and are unable to move beyond that point. They fail to recognize trouble ahead and are ill-prepared to meet that experience. This also defines the task of the hero/innovator – that of 'breaking the spell' before it is too late.

The trapped one

Prometheus chained to a rock; Odysseus stranded for seven years on Calypso's island; the Children of Lir trapped in their guise of swans; Rip van Winkle imprisoned in his years-long sleep. All of these are examples of *entrapment.*

An individual or organization can likewise be trapped – by repetitive ways of thinking, assumptions that stultify development, or by emotions such as fear or anger that drive people in wrong directions. Recognition of entrapment can lead to an overwhelming need to break out of it and move forward.

The shattered jewel

Another common symbol portrays some form of fragmentation that must be re-integrated. In a field lie a thousand shards of glass; put them together somehow, and they become a beautiful jewel. The underlying assumption is that a desirable whole is achievable from the scattered fragments.

Much valuable and potentially useful information and knowledge can be found dispersed through the far-flung network of an organization. Harnessing this fragmented treasure can be a daunting but worthwhile task. Defining the task as putting together a jewel from the thousand pieces of worthless glass can be a useful way of building and directing motivation.

The joining of opposites

In the great mythic stories, opposites are often exaggerated, polarities are made explicit. The purpose of this is to dramatize the differences that must be somehow reconciled or transcended. The story will tend to first play out these conflicts and oppositions and then show a way of travelling beyond them.

But most business cultures operate on exactly the opposite principle. Throughout the organization, the aim is to build consensus.

This, of course, is the desirable goal, but too often it comes about by simply suppressing debate about differences. In discussion, people look from the start for points of agreement, and tend often to self-censor thoughts that do not fit in with the general view. Those who raise awkward questions are often seen as rocking the boat, not as people who are helping it to move forward faster.

But a consensus that was forged on the resolution of differences, frankly expressed and fearlessly examined, would be a much sounder road on which to travel than one which merely reflects the least common denominator of agreement and sweeps away real and important differences without discussion and exploration.

Seed to a tree

Another of the recurring symbols of transformation involves the ideas of a seed that has the potential to grow into a tree. This is relevant to innovation because it evokes the process of change and movement, the process of nurturing the new.

A new idea is like a seedling which must be treated in quite a different way to a fully grown tree. It must be nurtured, protected, given tender care. Only when it is fully grown can it be left on its own to stand up to the forces of nature.

In any established organization there are many fully mature trees, providing market share and profit that were vital to the company. In the search for new ideas, the objective is to grow more of these trees. But they have had to be grown, and given the care that growing things require. All too often, however, new ideas are not given the opportunity to develop. These seedlings are compared with the mature performers. The expectation is that they show all the resilience of the fully grown tree at a time when they need a stake to hold them upright in the prevailing wind. Much patience and care is needed to nurture new ideas and bring them to fruition.

Death, rebirth and sacrifice

A final set of symbols has to do with death and rebirth and sacrifice.

The myths portray death and sacrifice as an essential part of birth, as opposite sides of the same coin. Yet modern corporations have sanitized the negative concepts out of existence. It is acceptable to talk about birth but not death, about building but not about sacrificing. People are not prepared to talk openly about the death of an idea, the death of a product. This in itself creates a resistance to the emergence of the new.

Still less are people prepared to face up to the need for sacrifice. 'We have what we hold' is often the implicit motto of an organization. This is one reason why a company is burdened with products and services that no longer fully respond to customers' needs.

But the mythic stories tell us that acquiring something new can often be achieved only at the cost of letting something go. The sacrifice is often a necessary stepping stone on the way forward.

6

CORPORATE RITES OF PASSAGE

The Rituals of Transformation

Heroic or Errant, do we loop
the loop or does goddess life
love the intensity of our tour?
– Michael O'Siadhail

CONTENTS

- Introduction
- Ritual and Ritual Practice
- Rites of Passage
- Applying the Rituals
- The Ritual of the 'Round Table'
- Corporate Rites of Passage

INTRODUCTION

For successful innovation to take place, there must be a meeting of individual and corporate action. On the one hand, the ideas of the innovator (hero) must be assumed into the structure of the organization. On the other, people within the organization (warrior, guardian, craftsman, king) must participate willingly in the subsequent changes, and help to move successfully into the future.

This chapter outlines a structure within which an organization is enabled to accept the ideas of an innovator and proceed with change, without irreparably damaging its heritage, its culture and its spirit. Again, as in the journey of the individual innovator, the world of myth provides interesting and instructive analogies, pointing to the redemptive influences of community ritual.

RITUAL AND RITUAL PRACTICE

The impact of Greek civilization on the world is beyond doubt. Its contribution in terms of architecture, politics, drama, art, philosophy and poetry has been truly vast. The Greek myths have been the source of inspiration for much of Western creativity. But as the classical scholar, Jane Ellen Harrison, has pointed out, these myths were based on community ritual. In time, the rituals, the actions were forgotten while the stories which were central to the rituals remained. It other words, the great myths evolved out of ritual. Ritual and ritual practice was at the heart of the Greek world.

Greek ritual, such as the Panathenaic festival, involved the whole community, including those otherwise marginalized, e.g. outsiders, slaves and women. Other rituals such as performances of Greek tragedy probably only involved men, and the fertility festivals were for the women of the community.

These festivals and rituals allowed the Greek community to step back from the day-to-day and address important questions affecting their lives.

RITES OF PASSAGE

Foremost among Greek rituals would have been the celebration of moments of transition in an individual's life (Fig. 6.1).

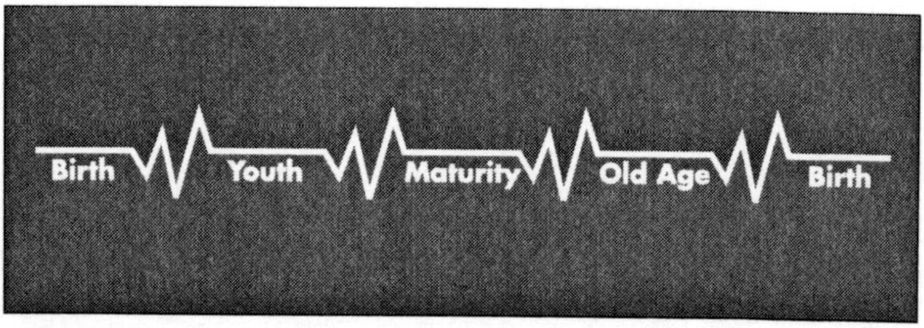

Fig. 6.1 Moments of transition.

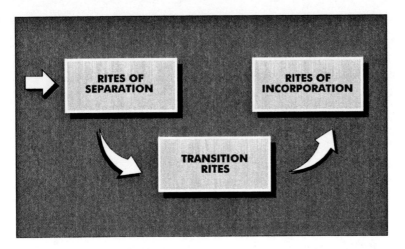

Fig. 6.2 The journey: rites of passage.

The anthropologist, Van Gennep, in his study of these universal moments, has highlighted three basic community rituals associated with what he terms the rites of passage: rites of separation, transition rites and rites of incorporation (Fig. 6.2). The whole purpose of such rites he sees as ensuring the transition from one state and stage in life to the next. The individual is initiated by the rituals of the community into a new social position, a new status as a member of the community. The community in turn is energized and enriched by the experience.

APPLYING THE RITUALS

Van Gennep's achievement in *The Rites of Passage* is, first of all, to establish the interconnectedness and universality of the rites of transition and, secondly, to draw attention to the relevance of these rites in the largely secular, urban world of today. This is a world which has very little experience of ritual and even less of 'community ritual'. Certainly we mark the pivotal moments of birth, marriage and death and perhaps view them as rare opportunities to step back from hectic day-to-day pressures and somehow reflect on the ultimate questions of life. But these are moments within the family, private rather than communal moments.

Van Gennep points to the involvement of community in ancient ritual, focusing on ritual as a means of accomplishing a social 'regeneration', of reviewing the energy of the social system. The ancient rites seem to offer analogies for developing a framework of corporate innovation; they seem to offer a way of involving the individual and the whole community in a corporate rite of passage, where a group can make the transition from one stage to the next, effecting real change, successfully.

Another anthropologist, Victor Turner, elaborating on the ideas of Van Gennep, points out the characteristics of those people who are caught up in the transition period. He reminds us that:

in order to live, to breathe, and to generate novelty, human beings have had to create by structural means spaces and times in the calendar. These areas of time and space – rituals, carnivals, dramas and latterly films – are open to the play of thought, feeling and will; in them are generated new models, often fantastic, some of which may have sufficient power and plausibility to replace eventually the force-backed models that control the centre of a society's on-going life.

He goes on to highlight the properties of the society during this transition state (liminal state) and contrasts it with the everyday hierarchically based status system. His list makes interesting reading:

In the transition state	In the normal status system
Absence of rank/status	Distinction of rank/status
Equality	Inequality
Silence	Speech
Acceptance of pain/suffering	Avoidance of pain/suffering
Foolishness	Wisdom
Unselfishness	Selfishness
Humility	Just pride of position
Disregard for personal appearance	Care for personal appearance
Simplicity	Complexity
Totality	Partiality

Turner also highlights the powerful bonding that takes place between participants during the transition state. He calls this 'communitas'. It is a period during which the group is closely knit and bonded together, having entered another 'temporary' culture, experiencing the 'temporary madness', the wonderful 'upside-down-world' of ritual practice.

THE RITUAL OF THE 'ROUND TABLE'

The Celtic myths of King Arthur and the Round Table are also applicable in dealing with the area of transition at a corporate level. Arthur's achievement was to unite the warring barons at a time of great strife and conflict in England. It seems that the Round Table was the event and place for rituals of storytelling and feasting, and which perhaps acted to hold the country together.

Most importantly, a noble convention governed the Round Table:

> *It was ordained of Arthur, that when his fellowship sat to meet, their chairs should be high alike, their services equal, and none was before or after his comrade. Thus no man could boast that he was exulted above his fellow, for all alike were gathered around the board, and none was alien at the breaking of Arthur's bread.*

– Wace, Roman de Brut

This non-hierarchical status is, of course, entirely analogous to the properties of a society experiencing the rites of transition so clearly highlighted by Turner.

We can therefore conclude that a combination of the wisdom of myth and story (the hero's journey) and the closely related wisdom of myth and ritual (the efforts and actions of a community) can provide the possibility of an integrated framework of action to ensure successful movement, thus achieving the desired goal of 'creating innovation and management of change which does not yet exist'.

CORPORATE RITES OF PASSAGE

TOWARDS A FRAMEWORK FOR BREAKTHROUGH IN INNOVATION

Every company, every product and every service goes through transitions, times when it must change from one stage of its existence to another. These transitions may be necessitated by changes in the outside world or by internal forces. In an individual's life, similar transitions occur, again necessitated by either internal or external pressures.

This framework is intended to outline what can be done to ensure that an organization 'manages' these major transitions. It will focus on 'who' needs to be involved, 'what' they can do to ensure success and 'how' certain key events can be managed for successful results.

Successful innovation requires that an individual (or creative minority) withdraw for a time from the pressures of day-to-day business to discover the possibilities of what might be. This process of discovery is outlined in many of the great myths and legends. It is what we have called 'The Hero's Journey'!

The ancient myths, by analogy, provide a road map for the hero/innovator, pointing out key landmarks along the way. The myths also indicate how difficult it can be to bring back that 'discovery' to the community for which it was sought. Many fail on the return journey: mythology is strewn with tales of 'dead heroes'.

In order to avoid such problems and to actually achieve successful innovation, an organization may set up an integrated set of innovation rituals that involves everybody (either directly or through representation). In other words, the organization, as a whole community, steps into a very different culture. It allows itself a temporary break from the day-to-day; it moves into a vital space to attend to the future, to birth, fertility and growth.

There are certain 'ground rules' covering such events:

- They must involve representatives of all levels and functions within the organization. The extent of involvement will vary of course and will be heightened at certain stages. For example, during the early withdrawal and discovery phases the hero figures/innovators are the key players. The bards, the guides, the king and/or queen and principal warriors are also very important early on.
- The particular 'players' should be carefully identified, using diagnostic tools or word-of-mouth recommendations; hero and bard frequently connect via an informal network; modern media makes this networking even easier. Such people tend to sense each other out and quickly form intense bonds of trust.
- The basic ground rule for every innovation ritual is that all signs of hierarchy and status are suspended. Being away from the office, informal dress, a relaxed environment – all help create a 'temporary' culture conducive to the idea of innovation.
- Round Table sessions should not be run by top management. Suspension of the day-to-day hierarchical pattern is essential. All are equal at the Round Table. The function of leadership should be divorced from normal corporate 'power'. An experienced organizer (possibly an outsider) can adopt the role of facilitator, analogous to the role of the guide in the mythic paradigm – the person who could help the traveller but did not make the journey.
- The model of cultural 'rituals of reversal' is important at such crucial points in an organization. Normal roles can be inverted for one day, so that those who give orders can, for example, serve food. This links up with the thinking behind the Arthurian legend, and has in fact been a pattern in such highly disciplined organizations as the British Army and the Roman Catholic Church. The carnivals of Venice promote the use of masks for the same effect.
- A successful exploratory session would preclude prepared presentations or memos written in advance. Only a very rough agenda would apply. The actual agenda would grow organically out of the event itself. The approach should be one of dynamic agenda building.

- Establish rigid 'process' ground rules (e.g. avoiding evalua-
tion for certain phases of the meeting). Ironically, it is vital
to be tight on 'process' (how people work) in order to create
a space for dynamic thinking on content. The well-docu-
mented techniques for brainstorming and creative thinking
are helpful in creating an appropriate climate.
- Leave space for storytelling as a way of sharing new and
different experiences. Listen and build on images and symbols. With skill, a 'living myth' can emerge spontaneously
from a group, a myth that is rich in meaning and power.
This in turn can become symbol-laden language which will
carry the team right through an innovation journey.
- Plan carefully the return journey, the coming back to the day-
to-day world of the organization. As with the individual
returning home, members of an innovation group coming
back with new ideas can experience the hostility and scorn
of those who have remained at home base.

THE FRAMEWORK: AN INTEGRATED SET OF INNOVATION RITUALS

Rites of separation: 'seeding ritual'

Too often, the beginning of an innovation journey is delegated
right down an organization, or even perhaps to outsiders such
as a new product agency. Report back, the brief is, when you
have come up with the Big Idea, when you have discovered
our future!

The 'rite of separation' is a different process. It is built on a
premise of collaboration, of community. It involves primarily
the kings, the heroes and the bards, and, of course, other key
players must be represented. But rituals have always been for
the whole community, so there must be a place for craftsmen,
guardians and warriors and indeed for marginalized people
such as scapegoats, fools and jesters. It will help if, at the early
stage, the chosen warrior/guardian types show some evidence
of hero energy.

The general purpose of this rite is to plant a few 'seeds' of inspiration, to articulate some general directions of exploration, and to build the vital network of contacts.

It is the specific task of the king to bless the journeys of discovery that are about to begin. And ideally to do so with an awareness of the challenges involved and with a promise to be there for the hero when the journey of discovery is over.

It is also the purpose of this rite to raise the consciousness of the hero to the prejudices, the mindsets, the attitudes and the assumptions of the key warriors and kings. This can be done first of all through the meeting of equals, using the principles of the Round Table. But secondly, and as importantly, it is through the stories of warriors and kings that the hero can learn of those formative experiences that will shape attitudes. Storytelling has an important place at the rite of separation.

The hero will be dependent on contacts, that supportive network of like-minded people. So the design of the event should ensure that as many connections as possible are made. The image of the kaleidoscope springs to mind here – the toy that shows patterns and is then shaken to show another, and another, and another! Yes, a kaleidoscopic Round Table perhaps best captures the appropriate process involved in this event.

Transition rites: 'first fruits ritual'

Two kinds of transition rite have a relevant place in the innovative process. These we can call the Fools' Round Table Ritual and the Implementation Round Table Ritual. While examining them, it is useful to remember all the while the Victor Turner characteristics of transition moments, the 'upside-down-world' effect.

The Fools' Round Table ritual
In a modern world the consumer is hailed as king, and so it is perhaps controversial to call the consumer, the fool. And yet, it is their 'fool' perspective that gives consumers their power, a

rich awareness that would certainly justify a full two-day transition rite where kings (and warriors) actually work with, and learn from, consumers.

The consumer is totally ignorant of company politics, of taboo subjects, of all internal prejudices. Like the naive young man in the Parsifal myth, like the child who sees the naked emperor, the consumer will say what comes naturally, what is obvious.

It is in this sense that the fool is so powerful, so able to break the enchantments that can blind a business, so equipped to say what no one inside the company can say.

The challenge to senior management is to sit with, to work with, to shop with, those whom they serve. It can be a humbling, shocking experience. It can be fun. Effectively, it can reverse the accepted world, showing up the king as fool and the fool as very wise (king). It can create an 'upside-down-world' temporarily.

For such a ritual, a guide can have a crucial role, shaping and crafting that special climate in which people feel safe enough to relax, to tell stories, to explore. The guide knows that behind every great product or service, is a great story. The purpose of this event is either to help create one, or to help others experience one that has been created.

The Implementation/Round Table ritual

Once the discovery has been made, once a Promethean character has stolen the fire from the gods, and it is time for implementation, another Round Table ritual comes into play.

Again, it is vital that the whole community is represented. An implementation return journey happens one thousand times if there are one thousand people in the organization. The involvement of different levels and functions within the organization, rather than merely the core project team, can make the return so much easier. In terms of key players, guardians, craftsmen and warriors are called upon to ensure effective implementation.

The guiding image for this event is the Japanese 'fasuma' concept. Unlike the Western house with its fixed walls, the Japanese house has internally moveable walls: they can be arranged to an infinite number of configurations.

And so it is with the implementation of innovation. Like 'fasuma', things are in a state of permanent flux. The target of the innovation ritual is to design this organization in motion.

In terms of sports language, implementation is like a shift from a relay race, to a rugby scrum, to a rolling maul. The maul is a somewhat chaotic affair with one side trying to wrestle and move the ball downfield. People fall off the maul and join again and the whole activity is in a state of total flux. The Implementation/Round Table ritual will no doubt at times answer to such a dynamic metaphor, and the renewed organization will likewise emerge in a state of continual flux and motion, unending self-organization, self-ordering chaos!

Rites of integration: 'harvest ritual'
The returning heroes and their discovery must in the end be re-integrated into the community. Each of the previous rituals has been set up to ensure the success of this process, the journey of discovery.

And so, the time will come to celebrate the return of the hero and the integration of the discovery into the mainstream of the organization.

The model for this celebratory ritual is drawn from the Irish Céilí (kay-lee). The Céilí is participatory. It involves singing and dancing on the part of the whole group. It allows for individuality as well as for group cohesion. The individual stands up and sings or tells a story, then sits back and becomes part of a wider group. Everyone is a hero for a few minutes as he or she shares a party piece.

These celebrations, these harvest rituals, are about people making their own entertainment. They are about ordinary people being extraordinary, allowing the individual to be a star and part of a team at the same event, thus reconciling two apparently contradictory needs.

THE FRAMEWORK AND THE HERO'S JOURNEY

And so, at last, we have a possibility of pulling together the powerful insights of the hero's discovery, meeting the enormous challenge of the return journey and ensuring that the innovative process can proceed within the group (Fig. 6.3).

The innovation rituals, which, as we have said repeatedly, must involve the whole community, can be judiciously imposed upon the essential hero journey process to ensure that the creative minority do arrive safely.

Like any discovery journey there is no guarantee of success. But the world of myth and ritual surely offers a wisdom, a set of guidelines, that very significantly increase the probability of success.

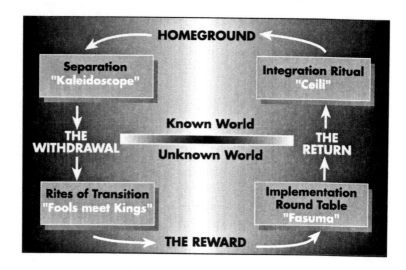

Fig. 6.3 The journey: coporate rites of passage, innovation rituals and the hero's journey.

7

THE APPLICATION OF MYTH

Myths of Innovation and Change

Watch over us on our travels
a saga of all that has happened
if we must be such wanderers
– Michael O'Siadhail

CONTENTS

- Introduction
- The Myth of Innovation (and Product Development)
- The Myth of Change

INTRODUCTION

The management revolution of the 1980s/90s was referred to briefly in Chapter 1 in considering a theoretical context for this book. This revolution is of course the 'Process' revolution, that shifting of the focus from permanent structures and systems to the more fluid world of process. This shift means a major move from 'what' we are doing to 'how' we are doing it.

We looked briefly at some texts from key commentators before focusing on historian Arnold Toynbee and his interest in the underlying causes for the rise and fall of civilizations.

In this chapter we seek to apply some insights to a number of recognizable contemporary concerns. It is intended to build on the conclusions of key texts and draw attention to the challenges faced in trying to implement their recommendations.

We explore the fields of innovation, strategy (especially third-generation R&D), change and leadership. We use the two meanings of the word 'myth' to structure these explorations – myth as that which is not true, and myth as embodying a profound truth.

❖

THE MYTH OF INNOVATION (AND PRODUCT DEVELOPMENT)

Without attempting to do justice to a number of excellent texts on innovation and product development, it can be said that there is a high level of common ground among them once the reader has struggled past differences in terminology. The texts propose a system which can be described as 'funnel and gates' along with a number of tools and guidelines for making the system work (Fig. 7.1).

The basic approach is to establish a structured set of phases for innovation and product development. Phase 1 involves creativity and the generation of a large number of ideas which are processed and developed into concepts for products or services or even process innovations.

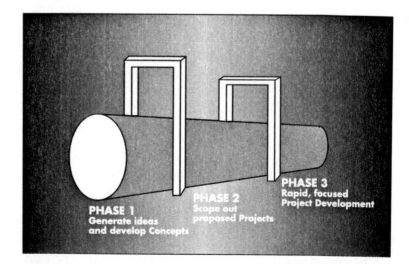

Fig. 7.1 Funnel and gates.

Phase 2 involves scoping out a small number of chosen projects in much greater detail and phase 3 involves rapid, focused, project development using heavyweight leaders and high-profile projects. A well-established set of gates is set up to screen the ideas, concepts and projects, and select winners.

In addition to this structure, a number of project-aggregating tools are used to establish the company 'portfolio' of innovation. The most commonly used is illustrated in Fig. 7.2. This matrix maps the level of product change on one axis and the level of process change on the other, to provide a framework within which existing innovation projects can be outlined. This usually reveals that the vast bulk of innovation effort and most R&D resources are focused on the safer aspects of product and

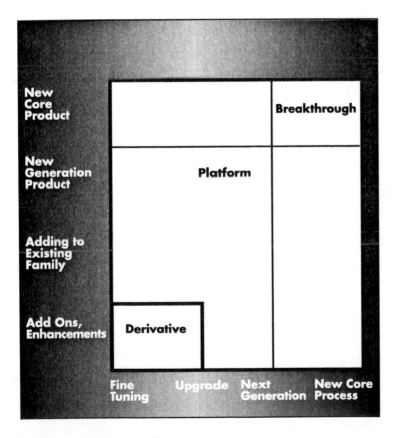

Fig. 7.2 Product/process change.

process innovation. What will also typically be revealed is that there are many ideas but none that are really 'big'.

Let us explore now the myth of innovation, using the meaning of the word 'myth' as that which is not true.

Innovation Myth 1: Systems and procedures will deliver 'big idea' innovation

There is no likelihood man can ever tap the power of the atom.
– Robert Millikan, Nobel Prize Physicist 1923

A company could skilfully adopt every possible system, procedure and tool and still fail to deliver any real innovation. Without a 'hero' figure willing to follow intuitions and journey into the unknown, there will be no real raw material to feed into the funnel. Without a king/hero similarly willing to support the unprovable as it matures there is unlikely to be the appropriate climate to grow genuinely big ideas.

It is only the hero or king/hero who has that passionate obsession with the unknown, with that which doesn't exist. Heroes are the heart and soul of innovation. Corporations tend to kill heroes while they create systems.

Innovation Myth 2: 'Ideas are ten a penny' or 'a dime a dozen'

Most senior people are reluctant to get involved in phase 1 of the funnel and gates because they feel ideas are very easy to generate. 'Bring me a big idea once you have it and then I will look at it', is a typical response.

Yes, it is easy to use creativity techniques (brainstorming, excursions, in–out listening, etc.) to generate a roomful of ideas. It is easy to use a variety of selection methods to screen these ideas. It is relatively easy to put concept boards in front of consumers for their initial response.

During the decade of the 1980s a total of 230 companies (46%) disappeared from the 'Fortune 500'

What is not so easy is to create a climate in the company that recognizes the value of the hero figure so that some heroes can exist. Nor is it easy to value their challenging, maverick, often naive, passionate, controversial nature. Heroes disrupt corporate life. They are not (short-term) corporate types.

Heroes are only interested in big ideas. They want to change the world. Their ideas are probably better called hypotheses and the reason they become big is firstly because they have been through many iterations and secondly they have developed outside of existing corporate mindsets and assumptions. There are actually few big ideas and few hero figures in most corporate environments. They need to be minded.

Innovation Myth 3: Senior decision maker can easily recognize big idea

The conventional innovation wisdom as articulated in the textbooks (e.g. Clark and Wright, *Revolutionising Product Development*) advocates the establishment of a well-defined set of gates through which the ideas and concepts are screened.

The implication is that the stage at which senior decision makers become involved is when decisions have to be made.

What is vital is the attitude they bring to these key moments in the 'funnel and gates' process. If they bring a warrior-like style (see Chapter 5), that may be very appropriate for running day-to-day operations; if they bring existing mindsets and attitudes which they are unwilling to question, if they are obsessed with facts and proof, then most of their behaviour will tend to have the effect of killing off the genuinely new, the risky, the really big idea. It will also tend to kill off the 'hero' who has driven them, hence the 'dead hero' phenomenon that is so common in myth and modern corporate life.

Wherever you see a successful business someone once made a courageous decision.
– Peter Drucker

The real challenge for the hero (and the open-minded king/ warrior) is to craft an opportunity for others to experience the journey that he or she has travelled. The hero (not the king) should set the agenda and style of the gate meeting. It is an opportunity to challenge, in a safe environment, existing attitudes and mindsets. The fool (consumer as fool) can also play a vital role, by being involved. The king meeting the fool follows the transformative ritual of reversal format where the world is turned upside down, the fool can become king and the king can see things from another, humbler perspective.

The 'holy grail' of innovation, the big idea, is not for sale. It will not emerge as a result of attending concept review meetings. It does not come easily. Kings, warriors and guardians need to travel the hero journey.

Innovation Myth 4: Consumers are good at recognizing big ideas (at first)

The choice for a politician is between a star and a hero. If you want to be a star you commission an opinion poll to find out what to do; if you want to be a hero you have to take risks.
– Shimon Peres,
Sunday Times 2
July 1996

Part of Frank Price's argument to the board was how poor conventional market research is at identifying new ideas. Frank listed all the new products that had researched well and done badly in the market (e.g. New Coke, Corfam, Ford's Edsel, etc.) and all those that had tested badly and yet done well (e.g. Walkman, Xerox photocopier, etc.). Market research professionals themselves are usually honest about the inability of their tools to predict, especially when testing the really new.

What this means is that relying on consumers to make innovative decisions through market research will likely mean a safe, known, preferred course of action.

Consumers, however, do have a vital role. They are an essential part of the journey. They keep the hero grounded. They can also, with help, become part of the inventive problem-solving, hypothesis-forming and modifying that is at the heart of any journey.

Innovation Myth 5: The emergence and recognition of big ideas is predictable

The structured innovation systems such as 'funnel and gates' imply that big ideas will emerge almost 'to order' as a result of following the steps, applying the screens, etc. Innovation, as in breakthrough innovation, is rarely as predictable as this.

No journey into the unknown is predictable. Big ideas are discovered, not made. The process of discovery works to its own logic.

Frustrating as this may be for a senior decision maker (king) who likes an ordered universe, that's the way it is. So what can decision makers do? What action can they take to progress this vital task of innovation?

Decision makers can:

- follow the passion (of the hero), not the proof;
- create a climate for innovation, not a system;
- stop talking innovation, and join in a real journey;
- spend some serious time with the fool (two days, not two hours);
- go shopping with consumers and see the world as consumers see it;
- spend the Christmas party talking to heroes, bards and the rejected underbelly of the organization;
- set up a ritual where normal roles are reversed or at least equalized (a Round Table);
- tap into the oral tradition;
- kiss a lot of frogs (e.g. half-formed ideas) in the expectation that one will turn into a prince.

A life spent in making mistakes is not only more honourable but more useful than a life spent doing nothing.
– G.B. Shaw

Innovation Myth 6: Increasing corporate visibility of innovation speeds time to market

The vital withdrawal phase is at the core of the hero's journey. The hero steps away from the homeground. This withdrawal is essential to enable the exploration of other assumptions, new ways of looking at the world. It is also essential in order to have the time to reflect. Space is an essential prerequisite of innovation. So is time to reflect and think. The day-to-day environment of most corporations allows little time to think. People are just so busy with the day-to-day. Increasing the profile of innovation can mean it is impossible to withdraw, because time, space and money are ever more tightly controlled, so the whole exercise could well be counterproductive.

To know much is not to be wise.
– The Chorus in Euripides' The Bacchae

Even as an innovation project matures, modern tools such as Lotus Notes can mean senior people stepping in, changing the specifications, tweaking the details. They want to know, to control. Visibility of innovation projects can unintentionally hamper speed to market.

Innovation rituals can be a powerful tool to hammer out details right at the start of an implementation journey. All implementors, be they on the core team or not, need the opportunity for early involvement. But this does not preclude the necessity for withdrawal, for reflection.

❖

The six myths explored above used the contemporary modern use of the term 'myth' – a myth is that which is not true. Let us look now at another meaning of the word 'myth' – a myth is a profound and enduring truth. Let us articulate a number of new myths for anyone concerned with the task of successful application of innovation in the modern world. It will be accepted that the word 'new' essentially includes insights which are also very old and timeless.

New Myth 1: Innovation as a journey of discovery

Discovery consists of seeing what everybody has seen and thinking what no one else has thought.
– Albert Szent-Györgi

The ancient wisdom of the world's great myths suggests we see innovation less as a system and more as a journey of discovery, a journey into the unknown. This journey is unpredictable, full of surprises, strange encounters, excitement and despair, ambiguity and paradox.

New Myth 2: Let heroes lead innovation

Heroes are the people who thrive on the journey of discovery and are distinct from most others in the corporate world who tend to avoid the journey. For the conventional, it is too full of uncertainty, apparent chaos, and professional risk. Let heroes lead the innovation process, particularly during its early stages. These, let us remind ourselves, are the people in the organization who are passionate, rebellious, reflective, emotional, idiosyncratic and often naive (politically). They are difficult to manage.

New Myth 3: Withdrawal from mainstream

The hero must, mentally at least, leave the day-to-day of the life of the organization. He or she needs space to innovate.

Heroes and their chosen creative minority need to get away from the pervasive assumptions, beliefs, experiences, attitudes and indeed the sheer business of the 'every day'. Their task is the 'discovery' of the Promethean fire, the elixir of regeneration, the commercial holy grail. The journey will be unique, a journey of tests and trials, strange encounters, ordeals, dragons and demons.

New Myth 4: The return journey motif

The world's myths, this book's narratives (Frank Price and Jane Lipman) and our own experience give weight to the enormous difficulty of the return journey. Many heroes do not often make it. The 'dead hero' motif is an ancient and modern story. Heroes have entered a world driven by different mindsets, experiences, people. They have seen great possibilities, a vision. These things are not provable. Heroes can enthuse, they can tell stories, paint a picture. But so many in the homeground believe only facts, proof, the tried and tested; hence the 'dead hero' phenomenon. Herein lies the real crux of whether innovation works or fails.

New Myth 5: Kings, warriors, guardians must travel

The key decision makers have to make some moves to help the returning heroes. Otherwise the odds are simply overwhelmingly against the solitary (or creative minority) hero. They need to meet the hero according to the hero's agenda, not their own, if the return journey problems are to be addressed. The typical boardroom is not a place for the speculative, the intuitive, feeling-based decision or for the new. It is a home match for key decision makers and an away match for heroes. Let heroes design the place, the participants, the process.

New Myth 6: Rituals to manage return

We have already explored how some of the world's most innovative communities sometimes used community rituals to attend to their vitally important long-term agendas (Chapter 6). For them fertility was a critical issue. Fertility actually seems a good word for innovation – it is about giving birth. At these

The fact that an opinion has been widely held is no evidence whatsoever that it is not entirely absurd; in view of the silliness of the majority of mankind, a widespread belief is more likely to be foolish than sensible.
– Bertrand Russell

All human progress involves, as its first condition, the willingness of the pioneer to make a fool of himself.
– G.B. Shaw

(innovation) rituals all key members of the (corporate) community would let go of everyday concerns to address issues vital to their long-term survival. An integrated set of rituals involving separation, transformation and return would constitute a potential formula for a corporate rite of passage. Other ritual processes find a way of reversing (or equalizing) the hierarchy of normal business life. Find moments in the year to create a 'world upside down' effect.

New Myth 7: Leading innovation – the master of two worlds

There are more things in heaven and earth, Horatio, than are dreamt of in your philosophy.
– Shakespeare

A great leader (as king) actually realizes that for a healthy business (kingdom) a number of very different styles of leadership are needed. Heroes will tend to lead the innovation agenda, with help from bards, guides, friends, fools, etc. Warriors win today's battle with today's tools with help from guardians, craftsmen. Both are absolutely essential to the present and future of a business. The great king is a Master of Two Worlds – warrior world and hero world – and also crafts integrating rituals to ensure healthy coexistence of the two, often contradicting, energies vital to corporate survival.

❖

THE MYTH OF CHANGE

A man of great common sense and good taste – meaning thereby a man without originality or moral courage.
– G.B. Shaw

Sing the Darker Muses of complexity.
– Michael O'Siadhail

There are many types of change programmes. When distilled down, however, a fairly common set of logical steps can be seen beyond the semantic differences. Once the scope of the programme and the approach is agreed, it will usually be followed by an analysis stage (questionnaires, interviews, focus groups, etc.) with the external world (consumers, customers, competitors) and with an internal focus (employees at different levels and functions). This analysis forms the basis of the change agenda and vision which is perhaps launched at some event/workshop, or even worked out with senior management. The real action happens after appropriate skill training when a number of change projects are set up. These are usually led by volunteers from within the business. They then have to lead a cross-functional, cross-hierarchical group to get results within some defined time scale. The change projects will be pulled together at a defined review and learning stage which sets up the process for stage 2 where further training and new projects are initiated. This approach was broadly that followed by Jane Lipman's company, Fifth Wave.

Now what can the wisdom of the world of myth suggest to help what seems like an evidently sensible, logical approach?

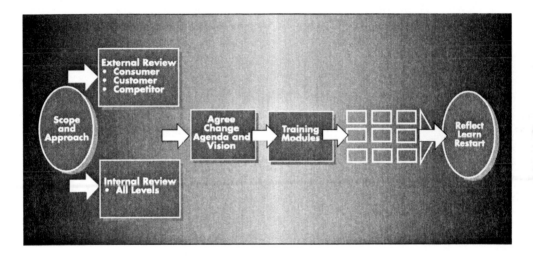

Fig. 7.3 A typical change process.

The real value of myth, as we begin to focus on practical applications, is that it moves beyond the formal logic of change programmes to provide an image-rich description of what actually happens and of the implicit, unstated agendas that people bring to change programmes. Most importantly though, it provides a non-judgmental language by which some vital things that block real change can be made explicit.

The following myths are based on the negative connotation of the word: a myth as that which is not true.

Change Myth 1: People want to change

Early in the withdrawal phase of the journey the hero finds himself face to face with a demon or dragon who must be confronted. This demon we can see as the demon of the 'no change' agenda, the embodiment of fear, resistance, ambivalence, laziness, unwillingness to let go of what we have.

So while it is relatively easy to commit to change as a concept or as an idea for others, the myth message seems to be that the real journey across the threshold of adventure only happens once the hero has come to an accommodation with the demon. Then the journey can continue into a territory of truly new experience.

It is possibly a good starting point to assume that there is at least as much energy in the change agenda as in the 'no change' agenda.

Change Myth 2: Yes means yes

At the start of any formal corporate change process it can be very politically incorrect to say anything other than a big 'yes' to the change agenda. To say otherwise can appear disloyal and uncooperative. To voice any reservations can be to place oneself firmly in the 'no change' camp and perhaps be described in language that would make the demons of the world of myth look relatively tame.

At a launch of a change programme employees will usually be asked to commit themselves to change and to 'making it happen'. What exactly does this mean? What does a formal and public 'yes' to change actually mean?

It is perhaps worth giving some thought to:

- the 'hero' characters who took risks on the last corporate change initiative, perhaps got burned, ending up as 'dead heroes'. They will be an unspoken voice of understandable cynicism.

- the 'bard' characters who have stories to tell of past initiatives. The track record of internal change programmes is usually mixed. Many fail. The internal oral tradition in a company will carry stories of these past change programmes, how starting is easy, delivering real results another story.
- the 'warrior' characters who know that working on change projects represents an extra task, a spare-time activity that can frequently detract from performance on the 'main job'. If you want a good appraisal, promotion, the response can be: 'keep your head down' and keep focused on the primary task.
- the 'king' character who *talks* change all the time but fails to realize that the king will be judged not on what is *said* but what is *done*. It is as if talking change is a way of avoiding actually doing anything.
- the 'fellow travellers' who perhaps should have sorted out the issue within their day-to-day responsibilities.

Me thinks he doth protest too much.
– Shakespeare

So while it is important to get a formal and public 'yes' from the corporation at all levels, the wisdom of myth would draw attention to the likely ambivalence in the formal 'yes'. The 'no agenda' needs attention.

Change Myth 3: Getting results (and the 'double Judas' effect)

In the early days of cross-functional projects there is usually a honeymoon period when the functions enjoy learning from one another. Ironically, problems can crop up when these projects actually start to produce results.

Most, if not all, of the participants in these groups are part-time members of the change project. They all have other jobs (and therefore other responsibilities and loyalties). It is possible to see each participant's involvement in the project team as a mini-hero journey. The participant's return journey can be painful. Change-project participants tend to behave collaboratively when in their project group without anticipating 'back home' reactions. These can be amplified if the boss is ambivalent or privately negative about the change agenda.

Either way, change-team participants can be treated as if they have let the boss down. But they can also feel, and be made to feel, that they let down the project team. Hence the term 'double Judas' effect.

Those who behave most collaboratively in cross-functional projects can end up very isolated as projects start to make progress. This can happen whether the projects are recognized initiatives in a decentralized multinational, cross-functional projects in a functional or matrix structure, or even innovation projects. It is almost as if the system conspires against the most enthusiastic and collaborative. There are too many people threatened if these projects are seen to actually succeed.

Change Myth 4: Tangible results drive change

Many change projects rightly focus on getting tangible results. After all, results are the essential calling card in most businesses.

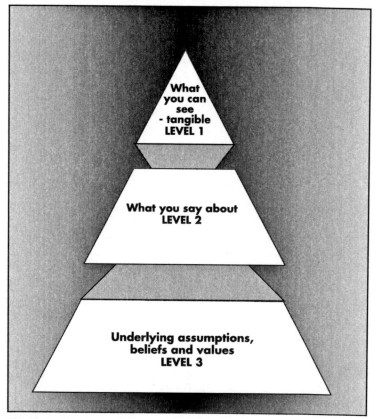

Fig. 7.4   Change myth 4.

'Performance is Power' is the driving maxim.

Some change models highlight the different levels at which change needs to happen in an organization (Fig. 7.4). Level 1 addresses what you can actually see in an organization – everything that is tangible. Level 2 addresses what is said about it and level 3 covers the underlying assumptions, beliefs and values. These are often an organization's 'unwritten laws'.

A tangible result-focused change approach will deliver lasting results only if the changes are explicitly connected to level 2 and level 3 change. Conversely, if level 1 results are not achieved it could well be because no change has occurred at level 2 and level 3. Lasting change is because it has happened at all levels. This is particularly difficult at level 3. It is at this level that 'myth' and a myth-based way of working is particularly strong.

It is difficult to get a pragmatic business group talking at level 3. It is even more challenging when senior managers think they hold a set of values and beliefs and yet their juniors think they act in a way that is significantly at variance with these assumptions. Or at least the 'effect' of their action is at variance with their stated intentions.

The use of myth, storytelling, rituals (especially rituals of reversal) provides a safe distance at which this vital area can be explored without loss of face or a series of dead heroes, dead consultants, even dead kings.

❖

The four change myths explored above were an attempt to de-mythologize some commonly held points of view. They were also trying to explore some of the complexities and subtleties of actually trying to 'make change happen'. The logical change programme outlined in the text is fine. It must, however, be complemented to make it work in practice.

Here are some 'new myths' derived from the arguments in this book. They are intended for anyone concerned with the successful application of change process in the modern corporation.

New Myth 1: Clear up the past

*And when I
heard Jimmy Jack
and your father
swapping stories
about Apollo and
Cuchulain and
Paris and Ferdia
– as if they lived
down the road –
it was then I
thought I knew –
perhaps I could
live here.*
– Yolland in
Brian Friel's
Translations

Attempting to change a business is not a new effort. Invariably in every company there are a series of past change initiatives. It is likely some of these will have failed and perhaps been buried (usually quietly). Others will have been only partially successful. Even successful change programmes are likely to have caused some collateral damage somewhere.

This means that within the organization there will be some 'baggage'. This could be in the form of 'dead heroes', who in some way are living on, perhaps wounded or cynical. There will be the 'bards', who through their stories capture the pattern of past change experiences. They will tell of what actually happened, beyond the 'hype' and the formal public statements.

If these past experiences are not dealt with explicitly, they will often play a powerful role, not always positively, in shaping current change agendas. In the context of myth/ritual discussed in Chapter 6, perhaps we can learn from the funeral customs of certain cultures. The Irish term for funeral is a 'wake', a term rich in its double connotation. The custom involves the 'body' being brought into the home. The living pay their respects to the deceased and reflect through stories on a life now over.

The wisdom of ancient myth/ritual would suggest the formal burial of past change programmes through some corporate 'wake' ritual. Dealing with the past provides the necessary empty space to wake up to a new future.

New Myth 2: Facing the demon 'no'

If a change initiative is supported at senior levels it can be very unwise to be anything other than publicly supportive. In essence, everyone says 'yes, we need to change', while corporate political correctness silences any other voice. On one level it is likely that everyone does agree with the principle of the need for change. What is most unlikely is that they agree on *how* to change. These disagreements are likely to be silenced as well. They can be interpreted as being against the principle of change. The 'no' voices then go underground.

The wisdom of ancient myth highlights the inevitable confrontations with the demon/dragon. We can surely see this as the demon 'no'. Those who question are often seen in that light. Mythical wisdom points out that there can be no real journey into the new until the hero confronts the demon, or in our reading of the myth, 'yes meets no'. And through the meeting, the parties in change find that actually there is much of value in the 'no'. In mythical language the dragon is guarding something of great importance. There is also a shadow side to the 'yes'.

It is only once 'yes meets no' or hero confronts (not kills) the demon/dragon that the real change journey can begin. To attempt to sneak by the 'demon no' is futile.

New Myth 3: Outsiders as guide (not hero)

A vast global business exists to help companies manage change. The world of consultancy is powerful and lucrative and it can be exploited positively or negatively. The hero journey model as explored here sees the company as hero, or rather sees the 'hero' as a company employee. In this reading the hero does have helpers. They are a vital resource to hero figures. But these helpers/guides are there to coach, share road maps, give tips/advice. They are not there to travel the hero path.

The other option is to make the consultant the 'hero'. The brief, then, to the consultant is 'go out there, explore the unknown and find for me the holy grail of innovation and change'. This route means that the consultant is the primary (even sole) participant of the journey of learning, getting lost, developing hypotheses, exploring the new. And, if he or she finds the 'grail', the consultant is likely to have as many of the return journey problems as the internal hero, especially with implementors, who may resort to the 'not invented here' syndrome. The consultant solution may enchant the kings. It will not enchant the internal hero, guardian, warrior or craftsman.

But 'outsider as hero' can work. Perhaps it is because outsiders bring with them the authority of wisdom. In reality it may be more that they bring the insight of the fool. Consultant as fool

'Very pretty!' said Gandalf. 'But I have no time to blow smoke-rings this morning. I am looking for someone to share in an adventure that I am arranging, and it's very difficult to find anyone.' 'I should think so – in these parts! We are plain quiet folk and I have no use for adventures. Nasty disturbing uncomfortable things! Make you late for dinner! I can't think what anybody sees in them,' said our Mr Baggins, and stuck one thumb behind his braces, and blew out another even bigger smoke-ring.
– J.R.R. Tolkein, The Hobbit

Look at a roster of the 100 largest companies at the beginning of the 1900s. You'll find only 16 are still in existence.

is perhaps as useful as consultant as guru. The essential problem is that if this route can become habitual, a company then loses its own 'hero' qualities, its own ability to give birth, to regenerate itself. Consultant as hero, or consultant as guide/magician/fool, is the choice. The myths of the world highlight clearly the implications of each choice.

New Myth 4: Results from 'people who don't work for you'

Somebody has to do something and it's just incredibly pathetic that it has to be us.
– Jerry Garcia, The Grateful Dead

Being in the king role means access to powers (and restrictions) not available to others. There are powers inherent in that role, institutional powers. Those taking a lead in change programmes (heroes) also have powers (and restrictions) not available to others. But they are not the powers of the king. It is likely that, in the context of the change project, no one formally works for them. In short, they have 'to get results from people who don't work for them'. We might call this the 'power of the powerless'. The hero has little formal power.

What the so-called powerless (in a corporate sense) do have is other powers. These can be described as:

- *Power of vision* – the hero will often be able to paint a picture that is compelling, exciting and meaningful. This vision and the ideas that it contains will often move individuals deeply. Many corporate statements fail to connect at a gut level. They do not touch the corporate soul.
- *Power of ritual* – the wise hero will orchestrate (with the guide's help) innovation rituals that somehow speak to the real issues, connect to more than the corporate 'mind' by leaving space for passion, humour, fun, magic, for making mistakes, reviewing past mistakes and for the exploration of what people perceive is actually going on (as opposed to formally going on). Innovation rituals which relax the hierarchy or perhaps turn the 'world upside down' are powerful tools that release the 'power of the powerless'.
- *Power of passion*– this is one of the essential powers available to the hero. It may carry little weight in certain corporate board rooms but it certainly does act to motivate and inspire.

Travel Back in imagination to the middle of the 15th century. Johannes Gutenberg has a great idea – moveable type – which he believes will revolutionise the art of printing. He is trying to persuade a rich friend and colleague (and one of the earliest venture capitalists), Johann Fust, to give him the money to make his dream a reality. How would the world be today if the conversation had gone like this?:

Fust: 'I don't get it Johannes. You say your new invention will speed up the production of books, and drive down the price?'

Gutenberg: 'Absolutely Johann. I believe I can set a page of the Bible in a day.'

Fust: 'Doesn't sound so fast to me. A scribe can write more than a page a day.'

Gutenberg: 'That's not the point. Once it is set, I can print hundreds of copies of that page in the time it would take a scribe to write out a single page.'

Fust: 'And then what? I've had my market research people do some studies. According to their findings there is next to no interest in the marketplace for books, no matter how cheap they are. You could give them away, and people would still not know what to do with them.'

Gutenberg: 'Of course they wouldn't. Most people in 15th Century Europe are illiterate.'

Fust: 'What do they need books for then?'

Gutenberg: 'They will learn to read, once they have access to cheap printed material.'

Fust: 'I'm sorry Johannes. I just don't see it. We can't invest in something so speculative.'

–Philip Dwyer, *New Media Age* 12 September 1996

New Myth 5: Avoiding the 'double Judas' effect

The real moment of truth for change programmes is not their initiation. It is the management of the various return journeys. The 'double Judas' effect mentioned above can come very much into play. Participants can feel they have let down, even betrayed, both their boss and their change team. The 'double Judas' effect is often a function of how much work has gone on in winning the commitment of middle management to change. But, if it does exist and is not dealt with, the company risks doing a 'dead hero' to its most committed, most willing to change, employees, and by doing so, rewarding those who kept their heads down!

New Myth 6: Return journey management

Projects are at the heart of most change initiatives. Whether these are externally driven or internally driven, the real test is whether they deliver results. To do so they must survive the return journey. We have seen repeatedly how challenging this is. We examined above the mini-return journeys of individuals. Collectively each project team must also deliver. This can mean managing, perhaps, 5–10 quite discrete return journeys, depending on the number of projects involved. Each one will pose its own challenges. And what is important is not so much 'what' happens but 'how' it happens. This is what will determine whether the change becomes another saga of 'dead hero', long to be told about in the corporate oral tradition, or whether it is time for celebration.

New Myth 7: Change the myth

Earlier in this exploration the various levels at which change needs to happen were explored (see Change Myth 4). Distinction was made between level 1 (what can be seen), level 2 (what is said about it) and level 3 (underlying assumptions, beliefs and values).

Level 3 can be described as the level of myth because it is really only through stories/myths that this level can be made explicit. Corporate stories are the means by which the truth about corporate assumptions, beliefs and values is passed on.

The wisdom of myth would suggest that if a company truly wishes to change, it must change the myth by which it lives. Or, put another way, without work at level 3, the level of myth, it is likely that old patterns will merely repeat themselves, because there is no vital change of assumptions, beliefs and values.

8

MYTH ON THE BOTTOM LINE

Ancient Principles for Modern Times

He was praying like that and holding on to the altar
When the prophetess started to speak: 'Blood relation of gods,
Trojan, son of Anchises, the way down to Avernus is easy.
Day and night black Pluto's door stands open.
But to retrace your steps and get back to upper air,
This is the real task and the real undertaking.
A few have been able to do it, sons of gods
Favoured by Jupiter the Just, or exalted to heaven
In a blaze of heroic glory.'
– Virgil, Chapter 6, translated by Seamus Heaney (Nobel
Prize Winner 1995) in his poem, *The Golden Bough*

CONTENTS

- Introduction
- Creating Innovation and Change is a Destructive Process
- Innovation is about Power and Politics (The King must die)
- Change is a Journey/Innovation is a Journey
- The Power of the Oral Traditional (and Storytelling)
- Perspective and the Cubism of Innovation
- The Hero is in the Organization
- The King's Ritual Task
- The Last Words

INTRODUCTION

The moment has come to step back from the journey and view
this excursion in a somewhat colder light. Visiting, or revisiting,

the world of myth is a heady experience, but it is nothing more than an interlude unless it gives practical insights that can be applied in the hard-edged business environment of today.

Hugh: ... I look at James and three thoughts occur to me: A – that it is not the lateral past, the 'facts' of history, that shape us, but images of the past embodied in language. James has ceased to make that discrimination. Owen: Don't lecture me, father. Hugh: B – we must never cease renewing those images; because once we do, we fossilize.
– Brian Friel, Translations

This final chapter ranges over some of the implications to be gleaned from the connection between the journey myth and the process of innovation. These, of course, are personal conclusions. The reader may quite legitimately disagree with some of them or, even more importantly, may discover other and richer implications in the world of myth.

The richness of the mythic world is such that everyone can draw his or her own dividend from it; there is no ready-made list of conclusions that can be taken and used as a 'to do' list. A true encounter with myth will enable each individual to draw a set of individual conclusions applicable to that person's life.

Here, not necessarily in order of importance, are a number of general management principles which can be gleaned from the hero's journey myth.

CREATING INNOVATION AND CHANGE IS A DESTRUCTIVE PROCESS

Management everywhere asserts its openness to new ideas. They even build innovation and change objectives into their strategic plans. Delivery, however, remains an elusive myth (as in myth meaning nonsense). One of the reasons for this, as we have seen, is that innovation destroys existing investments in power structures, in careers, in installed bases of power and in capital. It renders personal specialities, experience and skill obsolete. Those who promote innovation (heroes) and who return with the grail, boon or life-saving elixir will obviously present a threat to those who stand to lose in the short term as ideas are translated into successful change and, of course, prosperity.

It is no wonder then that existing power structures will act to remove the threat. Hence the 'dead hero' phenomenon that is at the heart of this book. The Hindu religion understands this so well in its central creation myth and its idea of reincarnation.

We see Vishnu in three forms: Brahma the creator, Vishnu the preserver and Shiva-Rudra the destroyer. Yes, if we want to reincarnate and preserve our organization over time we must look at creation and its sister, destruction. They are two sides of the same coin (or Hindu god!).

Making explicit the destructive face of innovation and change increases our likely ability to manage successfully the 'battle' for the future. As Toynbee, the Historian, reminds us, if Zeus (the status quo) does succeed in his anger to destroy the fire stealing Prometheus (a 'dead hero' in the Greek myth) we are, in the long term, condemned to the scrap heap of great civilizations.

INNOVATION IS ABOUT POWER AND POLITICS (THE KING MUST DIE)

If the new innovation is accepted, it will be because someone has some new learning, some new wisdom. These changes raise issues about territory, existing boundaries, future direction and strategy. Innovation and change may be sexy and topical. The shadow side is that certain people in powerful positions will not welcome it, in spite of what they say publicly.

This creates a central dilemma. Powerful people are saying one thing and doing another. They are also very resistant to any-one pointing out the say/do or intent/effect gap. They judge themselves on their words.

As we learned from Frazer's great work, *The Golden Bough*, the ancient way was to ritually (and regularly) kill the king. Sa-cred regicide was institutionalized to ensure on-going fertility and generativity. It was a key part of the longevity of two great institutions, the Egyptians and the Catholic Church. In the Church's case the king was not literally killed but the passing of power was institutionalized and automatic in many orders.

Today, we obviously do not have to actually kill (or fire) the king. But there will always be a death to old ideas, old beliefs and this at a very senior level amongst the very experienced, previously successful. It is very dangerous for the hero to assume that those with investments in existing power structures will be willing or able to act in the long-term interests of the organization.

CHANGE IS A JOURNEY/INNOVATION IS A JOURNEY

One recurrent mythical theme, as we have seen repeatedly, is that of the journey. And applying this metaphor to modern business, we see innovation as journey, change as journey, with all its implications of dynamism, surprise, excitement and fear. The traveller sets out with little baggage or possession, focuses on what is necessary to get through barriers (passports/money), tries to make new contacts to help on the way. The destination may be clear or vague and may end up being something that was not what was intended at the start. Some journeys are one-way tickets, others have a home base as the ultimate destination.

For any serious journey we need maps. This whole book argues that a culture's myths are just that map. We just need to learn to decipher, whether it be Greek, Chinese, Scandinavian, Celtic or whatever. The return journey poses its own problems of adjustment. Are we back to a fixed world again? How do we readjust and reconnect? How do we manage the battle between old and new and the journey's end?

Yes, innovation is indeed a journey, change is a journey. The ancient motif of the hero journey myth adds to our own experience of journey with its own particular timeless message.

THE POWER OF THE ORAL TRADITIONAL (AND STORYTELLING)

The business world tends to communicate important matters through writing. It is true of course that the written word leads to precision, accuracy and removal of ambiguity. It is vital for certain tasks. There are, however, other tasks that need to make use of the world beyond the written word, the world of story. There are certain things that cannot, and should not, be written down. This is the domain of the imaginative, poetic, even historic (corporate history). Such wisdom is often best passed on in story.

In short, if our task is the creation of that which does not exist (innovation and strategy), then let us give the oral tradition a place, a place on an equal basis with the written tradition. Let us resurrect the story.

Yes, myth is not as clear as formal logic. It is not as rigorous as physical science, but it does extend the range of things we can talk about. In innovation we need a place to articulate the gap between worth and action, a space to give vent to feelings, passions and intuitions.

Indeed, the oriental tale of Prince Five Weapons who takes on the ogre Sticky-Hair is just such a tale. For as the ambitious young prince finds every one of his weapons rendered useless, as it does indeed stick to the hair of the ogre, we find ourselves pointed to the whole world beyond the five senses. Each weapon represents a sense (smell, sight, touch, etc.) and we find a story pointing to the sixth weapon of intuitive knowledge that he has within. The young hero, of course, was the future Buddha.

PERSPECTIVE AND THE CUBISM OF INNOVATION

Cubism has been one of the great innovations of art, literature and philosophy in the twentieth century. Picasso, James Joyce and Nietzsche, through their work, give us a world view based on not one, but on multiple perspectives. The Chinese with their Eight Immortals, Eight Diagrams are just one small example of an Eastern argument for perspectivism.

It is the hero's task to seek out actively new perspectives and thus gain inspiration, make discoveries. But success is not automatically assured with discovery. Failure is the likely outcome of the return journey unless the hero understands the perspective of warrior, guardian, craftsmen and king. The hero must also single-mindedly hold on to and to keep alive the delicate 'flame' of creativity discovered on the journey. Gaining insight needs multiple perspective, but to return home successfully the hero needs to be a cubist, a beneficiary of multiple perspective.

THE HERO IS IN THE ORGANIZATION

One fairly widely held convention is that change must start from the top. Ancient myth would suggest that this is not true. In reality, very few top executives act as innovators. However, many of them feel that they should. They view innovation as part of their task. The mythical perspective suggests that the role of the king is to preserve the kingdom and hopefully to support the journeying hero. It does not suggest that the king should make the journey. After all, who would look after the kingdom when the hero is away?

A key leadership skill is to recognize, tolerate, even guide, the hero figures. It may also be their daunting task to save heroes when they are in trouble.

Top executives must realize that the innovator within the organization may be self-motivating, driven not by corporate directives but by an overwhelming desire to meet a particular challenge. Employees further down the corporate ladder must realize that they can be heroes if they so choose. They do not have to wait to get to the top before making the hero's journey. Indeed, by then it may be too late.

And armed with the wisdom of the maps of world mythology they can learn to die and be reborn many times (from the Christian myth), learn to be many faces and forms of the innovator (from the Hindu myths and the *Bhagavad Gita*) and like Arjuna:

> *Behold my forms by the hundreds and thousands – manifold and divine, various in shapes and hue,*

and finally learn from that arch survivor of the change process, Odysseus, how to get back home (see Homer's myth or the modern version in Joyce's *Ulysses*).

THE KING'S RITUAL TASK

It is not the king's role to travel the journey. (After all, who would look after the kingdom while he is away?) Kings do, however, have a vital task.

We learn from ancient scholarship of the intimate connection there has always been between myth and ritual, and this provides the focus for the final principle. The king's task at the start is to bless the journey. At the end what they can do is to create space for returning heroes via innovation rituals. These events, using the non-hierarchical format of the Round Table are places at which there is time and space for stories to be told. A story is the nearest thing to actually experiencing the journey itself. The king, if the king is wise, will allow the event to be crafted by the hero. This may mean some apparent chaos and it will mean the event does not run to the king's agenda, but it will create a space for the new to emerge and be experienced by those in power.

In a way, the king must die (not literally) but perhaps only for a day or a half-day and in doing so will realize that the hero's vision must be shared and developed by all those affected (warriors, guardians, craftsmen) by the new vision. Yes, ritual process is an ancient/modern vehicle to ensure a possibility of a successful return journey.

THE LAST WORDS

Let's leave the last words on principles to that Irish dramatist G.B. Shaw:

The Only Golden Rule is that
there is no golden rules

or the ancient mystics who tell us that while symbols or myths are powerful vehicles for communication, they are not the final truth.

So it is, then, while myth and story may have provided insight and wisdom, we do in the end have to transcend the symbol, the myth, the story and create our own innovation and change!

POSTSCRIPT

What do heroes do when they grow old? What do they do when they get tired of the abuse, tired of having their ideas stolen without credit, tired of investing themselves totally and passionately in what they believe in, for so little reward?

There are a few options for the old, perhaps tired, hero:

- Start another journey, and another and another. Indeed some heroes know nothing else, feeling that to move to any other place is to admit to themselves that they have failed, they have died.
- Give up on corporate creativity and become a social hero, a community hero, or the like.
- Move into becoming a corporate guide/magician, orchestrating rituals that help the next generation of heroes on their journey.
- Become a dedicated cynic and point out to anyone who will listen how unfair the world is (which it is) and how badly corporations treat innovators (which they do).
- Move into the corporate bard role and pass on through the oral tradition the tales of heroes past and heroes to be. Bards are the essential holders of corporate wisdom. They know how and why change happened in the past or why it failed to happen.
- Become the fool or the trickster and find humorous ways to upset the smooth order of the world and allow in some real insight.
- Importantly, and finally, take on the role of the king/hero. The modern leader will increasingly be the king/hero rather than the more familiar king/warrior. A king that once trod the hero path knows that the real task is the balancing of the

contradictory demands of warrior and hero, of the now and the future, of the known and the not known, of the bottom line (profit) and the top line (new sources of revenue).

Indeed, in the king/hero concept we have, perhaps a style of leadership for the next decade (or longer). We also have, perhaps, an ancient vision of leadership/kingship for modern time.

APPENDIX

Continue Your Journey Into the World of the Business Hero

This book is part of an ancient and yet contemporary debate as to what constitutes a heroic life. If you wish to participate in this debate, look up our web site:

http://www.businessheroes.com

- Enter into the debate and share experiences with others who follow the Hero Path in making corporate renewal their personal quest.
- Help build our story archive of heroes in business and how they manage to survive, even thrive.
- Particularly, share your experience of Corporate Rituals and Rites of Passage that are attempts to aid corporate heroes and keep alive the task of corporate renewal.

If you are interested in the debate on heroism outside the corporate world and in modern society, look us up at:

http://www.bard.ie

For commercial applications of these ideas in business, see:

http://www.alexanderdunlop.ie

Here you will find information on Corporate Renewal, Brand Archetyping, New Myth Development, Consumer Journeys, and Cultural Criticism.

Suggested Reading List

This is a very personal list. As you will see it is not a list of great 'business' books. It's somewhat more eclectic. These are merely some of my sources of inspiration.

- Aeschylus   *Prometheus Band*
- Jacob Burckhardt   *Civilisation of the Renaissance in Italy*
- Joseph Campbell   *Hero of a Thousand Faces*
- Edmunds (ed.)   *Approaches to Greek Myth*
- Euripedes   *The Bachae*
- Homer   *The Iliad*
- Homer   *The Odyssey*
- Machiavelli   *The Prince*
- Michael Murphy   *Golf in the Kingdom*
- Vincent Nolan   *Open to Change*
- Thucydides   *History of the Peloponnesian War*
- Arnold Toynbee   *A Study of History*

Again, personally, I like to adopt what my former colleague George Prince called the 'Hibachi Pose' – which meant 'proceed forward with a continual scanning of the world and the environment and trust that what is relevant will fall in your lap (or off your book-shelf!)'! Basically, trust your intuition to do the selecting – and then attend one of George's Connection Making Courses!

INDEX